INSECTS OF AN AMAZON FOREST

INSECTS OF AN AMAZON FOREST

Norman D. Penny
Jorge R. Arias

illustrations by:
Artêmio Coelho da Silva
Alberto Coelho da Silva

NEW YORK COLUMBIA UNIVERSITY PRESS 1982

*Clothbound editions of Columbia University Press books are
Smyth-sewn and printed on permanent and durable acid-free paper.*

Library of Congress Cataloging in Publication Data
Penny, Norman D.
Insects of an Amazon forest.

Bibliography.
Includes index.
1. Insects—Amazon Valley. I. Arias,
Jorge R., 1943–   . II. Title.
QL481.A45P46   595.709811   81-7665
ISBN 0-231-05266-9   AACR2

Columbia University Press
New York   Guildford, Surrey

Dedicated to our wives
Ana Maria Lira Penny and Kathy R. Arias.
Without their understanding and patience
this work would never have been completed.

CONTENTS

ILLUSTRATIONS

MAPS

FIGURES

GRAPHS

TABLES

ACKNOWLEDGMENTS

This research was partially financed by the following grants: CNPq's PDE-10-3-01 das Grandes Endemias; Instituto Nacional de Pesquisas da Amazônia (INPA, CNPq) projects 2017/103 and 2020/401.

The project could not have been completed without the help of many other people. We would like to thank Rui Alves de Freitas, João Ferreira Vidal, Altamiro Miranda Soares, and Orieta Catunda for their field support. A special note of thanks is given posthumously to Fortunato Sarmento Batista, who was killed by a bolt of lightning on November 16, 1978, while working on another study in a nearby forest.

Much preliminary sorting of.material in the laboratory was done by Cesarina Arcanjo do Nascimento.

Pedro Makyiama helped with construction of cages and furnished other supplies.

Finally, Dr. Brett C. Ratcliffe participated at the initiation of the project, offering valuable suggestions and personally carrying out the field and initial sorting phases of the baited pitfall trap part of the study. He has since freely given us help with the literature and specific details of the Scarabaeidae captured. To him we owe a large debt of gratitude.

INSECTS OF AN AMAZON FOREST

INTRODUCTION

The Amazon drainage begins its course 5250 meters high in the Peruvian Andes, winding its way down into a wide, shallow basin on its way to the Atlantic Ocean. Picking up water and sediments as it goes, this river travels 6437 kilometers; with a water flow of more than five trillion cubic meters per year at its mouth (Gibbs 1967) that pushes out to sea for 160 kilometers. Along the way, it has carved out the largest tropical forest drainage basin on earth, covering over six million square kilometers (Sterling 1973).

The Amazon Basin is not a uniform tract of monotonous forest throughout its length. This river basin, for instance, includes Pico de Neblina, the highest point in Brazil (3014 m). Along the Rio Negro tributary are large areas of white sand, where trees are stunted and epiphytes very abundant. As much as two percent of the Amazon Basin is seasonally submerged by overflow of the Amazon and its tributaries, forming a special, seasonal habitat (Goodland and Irwin 1977). The northern part of the Basin, near the Brazilian territorial capital of Boa Vista, is entirely open grassland for thousands of square kilometers. Finally, the climatic conditions are not uniform over the whole area, creating in the northwestern part habitats which receive almost constant, saturating rainfall, while areas in the southeastern part of the Basin are classified as semi-desert. Thus, the physical uniformity of the Amazon Basin is a myth.

The American tropics have long been considered an area of considerable biological diversity. In popular imagery, the Amazon Region is a teeming jungle where every tree and bush holds the potential for important new biological discoveries and the composite picture is one of almost unlimited plant and animal diversity.

Knowledge of some better-known groups tends to support this idea. For example, the region near Manaus has one of the highest concentrations of palm species in the world (Moore

1973). Pires et al. (1953) found 179 species of trees on three hectares of forest in eastern Amazonia, and Prance et al. (1976) identified 235 species of trees in one hectare of terra firme forest in central Amazonia. Klinge (1973) has demonstrated that these figures may be low, as he identified 502 species of trees and shrubs growing in a forest 2000 m² in Central Amazonia. As Kubitzki (1977) states "There is little doubt, therefore, that as far as green land plants are concerned, species diversity on earth is greatest in the wet tropical lowland forest."

The same richness has been documented for some animal groups. For example, within 32 kilometers of Manaus, at the mouth of the Rio Negro, can be encountered no less than 40 percent of all known freshwater fish species. Among terrestrial vertebrates, 40 percent of all known bird species exist in the Amazon Basin (Sterling 1973). With all this richness, the Amazon Basin has to be considered as one of the most varied ecosystems on earth, at least for these groups.

For most other groups of animals, relatively little is known. The INPA systematic research collections at Manaus, for instance, contain representatives of almost 500 families of arthropods, and this number will certainly increase with more study. The early naturalist, Henry Walter Bates, between 1848 and 1859 collected representatives of 14,712 animal species, mostly insects, in the Amazon Region, including 8000 new species (Bates 1962). However, these are just indications of great richness, and do little to quantify life in the Amazonian forest.

In recent years human development of this ecosystem has accelerated. Estimates of the amount of forest which has already been cut range up to 20 percent (Nicholson and Rohter 1979), and ecologists are beginning to speak out in criticism of forest destruction, using extinction of plant and animal species as one main argument. However, what do we really know of most animal species from the Amazon Basin? The larger vertebrate species are fairly well known, taxonomically. Of invertebrate groups, much recent progress has been made, but knowledge is still fragmentary. Early attempts to document the invertebrate fauna were mostly confined to isolated species descriptions. In recent years, many comprehensive taxonomic studies of individual groups have been published (e.g., Froeschner 1962;

Adams 1970; Stange 1970; Flint 1971, 1978; Costa 1975; Martins 1976; Val 1976; Richards 1978, among others), as well as checklists and catalogues (Carvalho 1957–1960; Kempf 1972; Penny 1977; Martins et al. 1978; Penny and Byers 1979).

From this taxonomic base, recent ecological theories have been proposed for several aspects of life in tropical American ecosystems. Haffer (1969), Vanzolini (1970), Prance (1973) and Brown (1977), using birds, reptiles, plants, and butterflies, respectively, as their research bases, have proposed dynamic models of speciation. They suggest that plant community oscillations over geological time have created forest and grassland island refugia for animals and plants with narrowly defined ecological niches. Janzen (1974) theorizes that large white sand areas, such as that of the upper Rio Negro, create situations where secondary plant chemical production is necessary, and this in turn inhibits insect life of both the surrounding land and water. Janzen (1966, 1971) has also shown interesting plant–insect interrelationships for ants and bruchid beetles. Janzen and Pond (1975) have used sweep net samples of secondary growth areas in Costa Rica, England and the United States to demonstrate that although the number of species is greater in the American tropical habitat, the total number of insects was relatively the same in the temperate areas as in tropical areas. Fittkau and Klinge (1973) have found that insect biomass of the central Amazon Basin is quite low, about 200 kg/hec/yr, of which about half is soil fauna; although as they state "the values have been derived from our general observations over the past ten years and from observations of others, but not from actual counting and weighing." Howden and Nealis (1975) have questioned this low figure for insect biomass, on the basis of studies of scarab beetles, utilizing baited pitfall traps near Leticia, Colombia. Saunders and Bazin (1975) have suggested that ecosystems with sufficiently high number of species do not show population fluctuations. Lotka (1945) has suggested that the reason for tropical ecosystems not having large fluctuations is the "damping out" effect caused by the many density dependent factors in the environment. However, Bigger (1976) has demonstrated several tropical insect species with large seasonal fluctuations, and Wolda (1978a, 1978b) has greatly expanded our knowledge of homopteran population fluctuations in Panama using light traps over a three year span.

Perhaps the best studied insect fauna in the American tropics has been the soil fauna. Beebe (1916) studied four square feet of litter near Belém in the eastern sector of the region and recorded the percentage of each invertebrate group, although only ants were identified to family. Williams (1941) studied the soil fauna of 11 square meters in Panama; the insects were identified to species, and the relative numbers were analyzed. Goodnight and Goodnight (1956) published the results of collections made in southern Mexico during the month of July, using various techniques, among them soil samples. Schubart and Beck (1968) studied the beetle families present in various central Amazonian soils during the drier part of the year, and Penny et al. (1978) studied the same beetle fauna for primary forest soils during the seasonal change from dry to wet season. Beck (1971) summarized much data on oribatid mite populations in different habitats of the central Amazon Basin. Willis (1976) sampled the soil invertebrates of Barro Colorado Island, Panama, over a full year and found strong seasonal populational fluctuations.

Erwin (in press) has described the evolution of "taxon pulses" originating in wet, tropical lowlands and radiating outward towards more temperate and arid regions. Erwin and Adis (in press) have suggested that short and long term inundation of wet, lowland, tropical forests are partially responsible for the great species richness originating from these regions.

The foregoing studies give frequently conflicting results, and analyze invertebrate populations for different areas, using different techniques under differing types of environmental conditions. But, do the insects of Amazonia behave like the insects of Panama, for example, where seasonality is perhaps more pronounced? Do theories proposed for inundation forests or white sand areas have relevance for the much larger areas of terra firme, laterized clay soils? A partial image is formed of the Amazonian invertebrate fauna, but the image is not clear.

In an attempt to help elucidate and augment our knowledge of Amazonian arthropod populations and richness, the present study was undertaken. It was planned to measure presence and abundance, at least to some degree, of all arthropod groups in a central Amazonian, terra firme forest over a thirteen-month period.

THE STUDY SITE

Ducke Forest Reserve is 26 km northeast of the city of Manaus (map 1), along the Manaus–Itacoatiara Highway (AM-010) known as the Rodovia Torquato Tapajós (map 2). The reserve of 90 sq km (map 3), belonging to the the Instituto Nacional de Pesquisas da Amazônia (INPA), is kept as a biological research area. Our site (map 4) lies approximately three kms south of the highway, and about 500 meters from the base camp's eating facilities.

Reserva Ducke was chosen because it is relatively representative of primary, terra firme forests in the central part of the

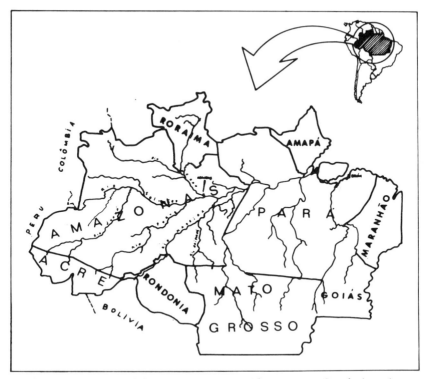

Map 1.   Location of the Amazon Basin with respect to South America.

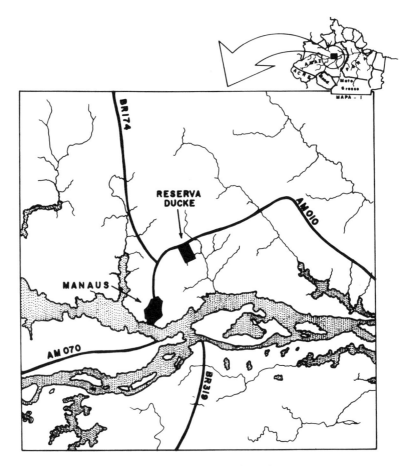

Map 2.   Location of the Manaus region and Ducke Forest Reserve (Reserva
         Ducke on the map) with respect to the Amazon Basin.

Amazon Basin, has had a considerable amount of background
work done on climate, soils and vegetation, is relatively free
from vandalism of trapping equipment, and is easily accessible
to us for weekly collections.

SOILS

The soils along the Manaus–Itacoatiara Highway have been
mapped to a width of 6 kms on both sides of the road. The
soils in the vicinity of Reserva Ducke are heavy textured, yellow

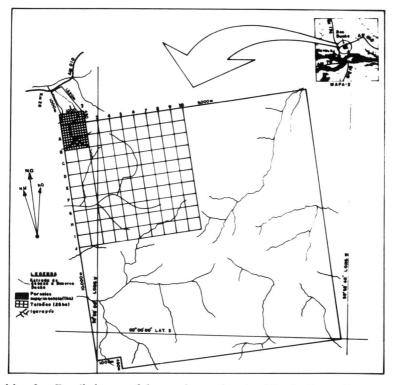

Map 3.   Detailed map of the northwest fourth of Ducke Forest Reserve.

latosols, and were described by Falesi et al. (1969) as follows:

The soils of the area in the Manaus–Itacoatiara region are deep, strongly weathered, excessively to very strongly acidic, of heavy texture in all profiles, the clay content of the B horizon varying from 50 to 70%.

The profile is well developed, having a sequence of A, B and C horizons. The A_1 horizon is relatively thick.

The dominant color hue of the B horizon is 7,5 YR, the root penetration and number of pores being distributed more abundantly in the profile than in the very heavy textured, yellow latosols.

The structure is weak to moderate, small to medium in form of subangular blocks, and the subsoil is less compact and less firm than soils of very heavy texture.

One occurrence, sometimes noted in these soils is the presence of an oriented line, formed by lateritic concretions, encountered at variable depths, and almost always located at the base of the B horizon.

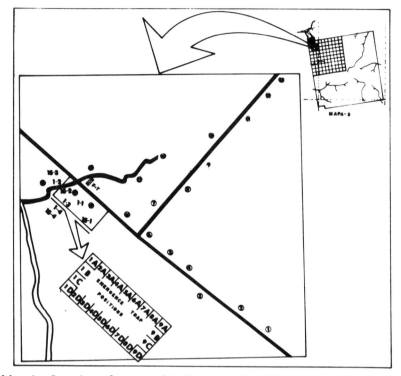

Map 4.   Location of traps within the study site with respect to the Ducke
         Forest Reserve.

These soils possess very low natural potential, evidenced by the
low saturation titer of bases and sum of permutable bases in all profiles.
The titers of organic matter in the surface horizon are high; however,
always less than the titers from mapped areas of very heavy textured,
yellow latosol.

The soils, herein described, always occur in terraces more or less
extensive and in varying heights of 20 to 30 m above the level of
nearby water courses.

The chemical content of the soil is given in table 1 (see
appendix).

The soil profile of these soils was described by Falesi et al.
(1969) as follows:

A_1–0–15 cm. pallid brown (10 YR 6/3); sandy clay; moderate; small,
subangular; firm, plastic, sticky; fine and common roots; many pores
and channels; flat and diffuse.

A$_3$–15–40 cm.; very pallid brown (10 YR 7/4); clay; moderate; small and medium, subangular; firm, plastic, sticky; fine and common roots; many pores and channels; flat and diffuse.

B$_{21}$–40–70 cm; yellow (10 YR 8/6–7/6); clay; moderate; small to medium, subangular; firm, plastic and sticky; fine and few roots; many pores and channels; flat and diffuse.

B$_{22}$–70–110 cm; reddish-yellow (7.5 YR 7/8); clay; light, moderately small and medium, subangular; firm, plastic, sticky; fine and rare roots; many pores and channels.

METEOROLOGY

In order to study the climatic factors influencing insect populations in Reserva Ducke during 1977–1978, it was necessary to study the normal meteorological parameters and whether this time period had normal or abnormal climatic conditions. This was done by analyzing long-term meteorological records for the area and then comparing them with measurements of some meteorological parameters taken during the study. We are indebted to the Meteorological Department of INPA, headed by Sra. Maria de Nazaré G. Ribeiro, for information on both aspects of meteorology at Reserva Ducke. Further thanks are tendered to Dr. Wolfram Franken for hydrological information gathered during 1976–1977 in the Igarapé Barro Branco drainage of Reserva Ducke as part of a long-term research agreement between INPA and Max-Planck Institute of Limnology, Plön, West Germany.

Further information was obtained by placing recording equipment in the forest at the study site, both at 1 m and 15 m heights. This equipment recorded constant temperature, humidity, and barometric pressure.

Insolarity

The INPA meteorological station at Reserva Ducke has recorded a monthly average insolarity between 1965 and 1977 of 153.7 hours. During the period from September 1977, to September 1978, the average hours of insolarity per month was 140.9, indicating a slightly below average insolarity for the time period covered in the study. Graph 1 indicates average insolarity by month during the period 1965 to 1977 and during the study.

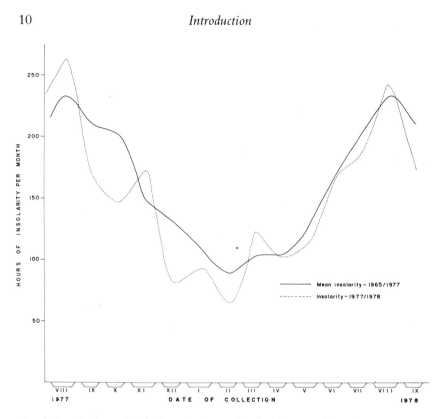

Graph 1. Average insolarity at Reserva Ducke, by months.

However, studies by Williams et al. (1972) in terra firme forest of the Rio Negro drainage indicate that only 1.1% of sunlight reaches the forest floor; the rest being intercepted by the foliage.

Brinkman (1971) found that in Reserva Ducke terra firme forest the majority of light wave-lengths were in the range of 5920Å–7500Å, with secondary peaks between 4420Å–6440Å and 3500Å–5150Å. He also found that before 10 a.m. 94% of the light intensity was below 200 Lux, rising to 65% intensity between 200 and 400 Lux between 10 a.m. and 2 p.m., and finally falling again to 66% intensity below 200 Lux between 2 p.m. and 6 p.m. A large percentage of this light came as temporary "sunflecks."

Readings as high as 5800 Lux were recorded for these temporary "sunflecks" in the forest.

Relative Humidity

The monthly average relative humidity (RH) at the Reserva Ducke meteorological station between 1965 and 1977 was 89.1%. During the period from September 1977, to September 1978, the RH averaged 87.1%, indicating slightly below average RH during the study.

At the study site itself, RH at 1 m was nearly always about 100% at 10 a.m., dropping to a minimum of 67–85% at about 4 p.m., then slowly rising throughout the night and early morning hours. At 15 m, RH was significantly lower (P < .001), reaching a maximum of 90–97% at about 10 a.m., then sharply falling to about 40–50% during the afternoon hours. After 6 p.m. the RH in the forest canopy quickly returned to early morning levels of 90 to 97%. Thus, seasonal fluctuations in RH, as recorded in an open area at the meteorological station, probably did not well represent the daily cycle within the forest, which daily attained 100% RH at ground level and 90% RH in the canopy.

Piche Evaporation

The monthly average piche evaporation (PE) at the Reserva Ducke meteorological station between 1965 and 1977 was 59.2 mm water. During the period from September 1977, to September 1978, the PE averaged 60.8 mm water indicating near normal evaporation rates.

Ribeiro and Villa Nova (1979) indicate the evapotranspiration potential at Reserva Ducke to be between 115 and 142 mm/mo, and that rainfall and ground water compensate for this evapotranspiration, except during the months of August to October, when there is a small deficit of 19 to 42 mm/mo.

The study site is within the watershed of the small Igarapé Barro Branco, about 500 m from the stream itself. A study conducted by Dr. Wolfram Franken of the hydrology of this basin during 1976–1977 has given a much better idea of water movement within the area. Approximately 21% of the rainfall falling over the study site is lost to runoff into the Igarapé Barro Branco, which has a normal water flow of 5 to 15 liters/sec. However, during heavy rains as much as 95% of rainfall flows directly into the stream which increases its flow to 600 liters/sec. A further 5 to 10% of all water leaves the surface flow system by percolating into the ground water system below. The other 69 to 74% of all water is returned to the air by means of evapotranspiration. Of this evapotranspiration, 40% is transpiration and 60% is evaporation. Thus, about 28% of all rainfall is directly returned to the air by way of plant transpiration (Franken 1979 and personal communication).

Barometric Pressure

The monthly average barometric pressure (BP) at the Reserva Ducke meteorological station between 1965 and 1977 was 752.2 mm Hg; and never varied more than 2 mm from this figure.

Precipitation

The INPA meteorological station at Reserva Ducke recorded a monthly average of 191.8 mm precipitation between 1966 and 1978, thus being 2301.6 mm precipitation per annum. The monthly averages for 1977 (202.9 mm) and 1978 (188.9 mm) are not significantly different from 1966 to 1978, with one being slightly higher, the other slightly lower than average. The yearly rain cycle follows a pattern of high rainfall from January to May, then tapering off between July and October. September has the lowest monthly average rainfall (91.2 mm), but yearly fluctuations are great (6.8 to 167.9 mm). Graph 2 indicates monthly average precipitation and precipitation during the interval of the study.

Franken (1979) has found that much of the rainfall in the area comes in the form of light rains. During 1976–77 there were 72 rains of over 5 mm. Of these 72 rains, only 6% were of more than 50 mm.

Temperature

Average monthly temperatures at the Reserva Ducke meteorological station between 1966 and 1977 were 25.7°C., fluctuating only 0.6°C. from this norm. High and low monthly mean temperatures for the same period were 36.6°C. and 15.1°C., respectively. Average monthly temperatures during the study were 24.8°C., fluctuating 1.5°C. from this norm.

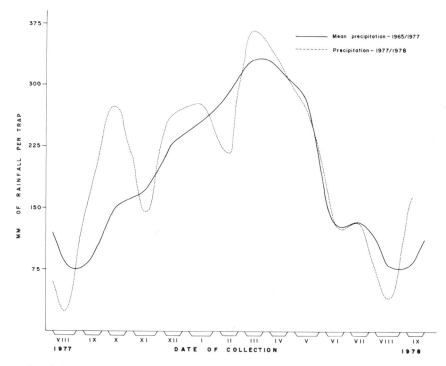

Graph 2. Average precipitation at Reserva Ducke, by months.

High and low daily temperatures recorded were 36.5°C. and 16.0°C., respectively. Temperatures during the study were significantly lower (Fs = 61.378) than during the previous twelve-year average.

Within the forest, temperatures were considerably moderated. At 1 m height, temperatures varied in a daily cycle from a minimum of 18°C. to a maximum of 28°C. In the forest canopy (15 m height), temperatures were somewhat elevated, fluctuating between minima of about 20°C. to maxima of 33°C.

VEGETATION

Central Amazonian terra firme forest is not a uniform mass of vegetation covering millions of square kilometers; it is quite variable (Prance 1977). Prance suggested division of the Amazonian flora into seven sectors; Reserva Ducke is located in the

Manaus sub-sector. He further described this sub-sector as
being an area of high endemism.

Probably the first attempt to quantitatively describe the Reserva Ducke flora was made by Lechthaler (1956). He surveyed
trees of over 8 cm diameter at breast height over an area of one
hectare and found 745 trees of 76 species. Of these trees, 117
individuals, or 15.7%, were one species of Burseraceae. Takeuchi (1961) working at km 42 along the same highway found
that tree dominance varied according to topography ("high,"
"low," and "inclined" terra firme). In the "high" terra firme
forest, the herbaceous layer consisted of *Trichomanes, Adiantum,
Asplenium, Ananas, Bromeria, Smilax, Plylodendron, Marantha-
ceae, Cyperaceae, Orchidaceae* and *Strychnos*. The lower tree level
was dominated by palms. The emergent vegetation was predominantly (41–54%) trees of the families Leguminosae, Lecythidaceae and Sapotaceae. It is interesting that Takeuchi found
Burseraceae to be the dominant tree family in "inclined" terra
firme forest, indicating that Lechthaler's earlier work may have
been done predominantly in this type of forest. Prance et al.
(1976) surveyed the terra firme forest of one hectare at km 30
of this same highway and found 179 species of trees of more
than 15 cm diameter. *Eschweilera odora* (Poepp.) Miers (Lecythidaceae) was the dominant tree species (7.4%). The most
common 11 species accounted for 25.4% of the total number
of trees. Almost half of the trees (45.1%) in the area produced
latex, resins, oils and phenolic compounds, presumably as a
defensive mechanism against insect damage.

TRAPPING TECHNIQUES

The number of habitats in which insects exist in a tropical rain
forest is almost unlimited. Special trapping techniques could
be devised to collect almost all of these species, but the amount
of time and effort involved would be enormous. The problem
then becomes one of maximally sampling the insect fauna given
the limited amount of time, finances, and manpower available.
Grimm et al. (1974) have considered this same problem for
sampling a temperate beech forest fauna and devised a minimum
trapping program to achieve maximum results for insect abun-

dance and richness. Their results indicate that pitfall traps, ground photo-eclectors, and arboreal photo-eclectors would achieve this result. However, these techniques are minimal and fail to indicate presence or abundance of insects which remain in the forest canopy, insects actively flying through the forest, and insects which exist solely in the soil. Therefore, we chose to initiate a program of collecting arthropods over a 13-month period, utilizing five trapping techniques: C.D.C. (Center for Disease Control) miniature light traps at two heights, ground photo-eclectors (emergence traps); soil litter samples, a flight trap, and baited pitfall traps (fig. 1). Samples would be collected each week, and specimens later sorted and identified. The last week's catch (3 Oct. 1978) would be counted, dried, and weighed, for an estimate of arthropod biomass.

C.D.C. *Miniature Light Traps* (modified)

These small light traps (fig. 2) consist of a small light bulb and fan combination within a plastic casing. Energy is supplied by an attached 6 volt, rechargeable, motorcycle battery. The trap

Figure 1. Schematic representation of the traps utilized during the Reserva Ducke project.

Figure 2.   C.D.C. miniature light trap.

is covered by a circular aluminum hood and insects are actively
sucked into a fine mesh, screen bag below. A wire grid covers
the trap casing, thus restricting entrance of large insects. A
styrofoam box (14 × 11 × 7 cm) filled with about 800 gm of
dry ice (solid CO_2) was taped to the plastic trap casing. When
filled with dry ice, the box was taped shut, so that release of
vapors was slow, normally being released over about a 15-hour
period. Traps were placed about 5:30 p.m. one day a week,
usually Monday, and were collected about 9:00 a.m. the next
morning. Usually a small pellet of dry ice still remained in the
box at this recovery time. The bags with the live insects inside

were then transported to the laboratory, where they were pre-served in 70% EtOH. Four traps were normally utilized, 2 at 1 m height and 2 others at 15 m, in the same general area. The same site was used each week from 1 Aug. 1977, until 3 Oct. 1978.

To study the possible effects of continuously collecting the same area every week, on three occasions during the study a double complement of traps was used; that is, an additional four traps were placed in nearby areas. These double trap catches were continued each time the original four traps were used during the months of November–December 1977; May 1978; and September 1978. Graphs used in the text have elongate bars to indicate months where double the number of traps were used.

Results of double trapping indicate that there was no signif-icant effect (Fs = 3.216) on monitored families in general by use of the traps over an extended period of time.

Gruner (1975) has demonstrated that light trap captures of some species of Scarabaeidae are strongly influenced by moon phase. We found no such cyclic nature to light trap catches for any of the families monitored. Our findings of moon phase having no effect on light trap capture may be due to placing these traps directly in the forest. If studies by Williams et al. (1972) on sunlight can be extrapolated to moonlight, only about 1% of moonlight would reach the forest floor. Thus, moonlight would have only a minimal effect within the forest itself. How-ever, light traps in the forest canopy also showed no effect.

This type of trap is used primarily to catch small, flying insects, especially Diptera attracted to CO_2. Many zoophilic species were thus collected. The traps were not good indicators for non-flying arthropods, arthropods not attracted to light or CO_2, or large insects (which could not get past the wire grid).

Ground Photo-Eclectors

Immatures of many groups of insects live in soil, humus, or litter material. Upon emergence as adults, they are either pos-itively phototactic or negatively geotactic. The result is the same; they rise out of the surface layer, either climbing or flying, to begin the reproductive and dispersal phase of life. To trap this segment of the insect community, ground photo-eclectors, slightly modified from those of Funke (1971) were utilized.

The soil eclectors, or soil emergence traps, are of two shapes, round and square. All enclose a soil surface of one square meter. The traps are comprised of a black acrilic or gray plastic base. The insides of these bases were painted black and sprinkled with sand while still wet to make an otherwise smooth surface rough and thus, presumably, easier for the movement of arthropods. A cloth funnel, which is supported by metal rods on the sides and a metal ring on the top, tapers to the collection cup at the top of the traps; this collection cup is a plastic container with a PVC (polyvinyl chloride) pipe through the center. The inside of the plastic pipe was also painted black and sprinkled with sand. The plastic collection containers were partially filled with a 5% saturated picric acid solution.

Within each of these emergence traps were placed an unbaited pitfall trap, which consisted of an eight oz. plastic cup partly filled with picric acid solution. These pitfall traps were used to collect emerging arthropods which seldom or never fly, or crawl to the top collector.

Three of these traps were set each month, placed over a 3600 m^2 area. This area (90 m × 40 m) was subdivided into 36 squares of 100 m^2 each. An area of 100 m^2 was chosen to allow us some flexibility in choosing an area where there were no standing or fallen trees or other obstacles. Each month, for nine months three of these plots were used for traps, having been previously selected using random number tables. Map 4 shows the 3600 m^2 area with the position of the traps.

Once a site was selected for an eclector, the standing underbrush was severed at 20 to 50 cm from the ground. Once in place, the sides of the eclector were sealed from the outside by the use of nearby soil. Care was maintained so that no disturbance occurred to the area where the trap would be set.

New eclectors were set on the first day of each month. The collection containers were removed and processed once every week, on Monday or Tuesday. Once in place, a trap was maintained throughout the study. Thus, some traps were in place over the same square meter of ground from 1 Sept. 1977 until

3 Oct. 1978. Others were in place for only 22 weeks. Cloth funnels were replaced constantly, as soon as a perforation was noted.

A general trend was noted from collections of all traps. An initially large richness and quantity of material gradually diminished in both numbers and richness. However, some families, most notably Scolytidae (Coleoptera), maintained population levels steady within the trap over long periods of time.

We found three unsatisfactory aspects to this trapping technique. First, there was the possibility that the trap acted as a micro-habitat for some arthropods, such as Collembola, free from normal predation. Second, we found that occasionally army ants would burrow a small hole under the side of the trap and be collected in the trap in numbers far in excess of normal levels for one square meter. Finally, after rains small pools of water would form near the base of the cloth funnel if they were not maintained absolutely tight. After months of exposure to the combination of high temperatures and moisture, an occasional cloth funnel would tear, releasing the contents of the small pool into the trap. This is the only way we can account for the single specimen of the aquatic beetle family Noteridae being collected in one of the emergence traps.

Soil Litter Samples

Soil and litter samples were collected per week to obtain arthropods extracted with the help of Berlese-Tullgren funnels. Four samples were collected within each 100 m^2 plot where the eclectors of each month were set. As there were three such sites selected each month, a total of 12 samples were obtained.

Each sample was taken with the aid of a 48 cm^2 rectangular metal box, open at top and bottom. After placing this on a spot of previously undisturbed forest floor, a knife was used to cut along the edges. Once the sampler had been pushed 2.5 to 3 cm into the ground, the sampler and samples were carefully removed, and the sample was placed in a plastic bag. These plastic bags were placed in a styrofoam ice chest and transported to the laboratory where they were placed in the Berlese-Tullgren funnels. Arthropods driven out of the drying sample fell into a small container of 70% EtOH. Samples were left until

completely dry, usually four days before arthropods were removed and processed. This sampling method was terminated
after 19 weeks due to a pausity of collected material, and difficulty of access to sorting equipment. Results of the beetle
collections can be found in Penny et al. (1978).

Flight Trap

This trap (fig. 3), which is a modified Malaise trap or Townsend
trap, was set on the first of September. It is used to capture
insects flying through the forest, which upon enountering an
obstacle tend to fly upwards. The cloth roof then acts as a
second barrier guiding them into the mouth of the collector.
The collector was the same as described for emergence traps
and the fluid preservative was a 5% chloral hydrate solution.
The original trap measured 3 m × 2 m and had a collector at
only one end. This trap was donated by the Department of
Invertebrates at Museu Paraense Emilio Goeldi, Belém, Pará.
This trap did not withstand the continuous high humidity and
temperatures and by the end of January 1978, had to be replaced.

Figure 3.   A flight trap.

Not completely satisfied with the original design, the new flight trap which replaced the old one measured 6 m × 3 m and had collectors at both ends of the roof. Although the modifications make direct comparisons between catches in the two traps impossible, the modifications were felt necessary due to the small size of original catches. On graphs of flight trap catches, a solid vertical line represents where the original trap was replaced.

One disadvantage of flight traps is that they work on the principle of insects rising when they encounter an obstacle. Some insects, such as Scarabaeidae, do not rise, but fall, thus avoiding capture. Many insects enter the trap, not by flying, but rather by crawling up the sides. Thus, some wingless arthropods were collected each week.

Baited Pitfall Traps

In a tropical forest ecosystem, available-protein is often a scarce or sporadically encountered food source for saprophagous arthropods, or females needing protein for egg production. Many arthropods have become highly specialized in detecting chemical odors emitting from these protein sources from long distances. Thus, traps baited with a good protein source can attract quite a variety of these specialized feeders. To attract this group of insects, two different baits—fish and human feces—were used. Each bait was placed weekly in ten traps, five with 5% picric acid solution as killing-preservative agent, and five with 5% chloral hydrate as killing-preservative agent. The total of 20 traps were arranged in a cross-pattern with alternating baits and preservatives. Adis (1979b) has discussed many of the problems associated with use of pitfall traps, and we have tried, wherever possible, to avoid these "pitfalls."

The traps were placed in the following manner: a hole dug in the ground was lined with a short piece of PVC pipe to support the walls. Into this was placed a one liter screw cap polyethylene jar which contained approximately 100 ml of the corresponding killing-preservative solution in the bottom. A small one oz. vial was suspended on the side of the jar. This vial contained the fish or feces bait. A square board, 400 cm² with circular hole in the top to accommodate the mouth of the bottle was placed across the top. All the pitfall traps had a 400 cm^2 plastic roof to impede rain from entering. All pitfall traps were set and collected every Tuesday, from 13 Sept. 1977 until 3 Oct. 1978.

Dr. Brett C. Ratcliffe was responsible for setting up the design and making the weekly collections of baited pitfall traps, as part of a study of Amazonian Scarabaeidae. The material was then turned over to us for sorting, as soon as the scarab beetles had been removed. He is greatly thanked for this effort.

Biomass

During the 13-month duration of the study, arthropods were sorted and number of specimens from monitored groups recorded. However, this method of recording does not give a complete representation as to the total impact of these arthropods on the tropical ecology. For instance, in the baited pitfall traps, the beetle family Ptiliidae was recorded much more frequently than the beetle family Scarabaeidae. However, the larger size and quantity of energy consumed make the Scarabaeidae a highly significant part of tropical ecosystem energy flow. Therefore, to get an estimate of arthropod biomass being collected, the last week of the study, in addition to counting the numbers present, the dry weight for all groups was also recorded.

To find the dry weight biomass of individual groups in each trap, insects were sorted, counted, recorded, and placed in small aluminum candy cups. These candy cups had been previously weighed on a precision balance to 0.1 mg. The candy cups and insect occupants were placed in a numbered matchbox, and this matchbox was then placed in a drying oven at 50°C. for one to three weeks. Matchboxes were used to allow stacking in the oven, to prevent accidental loss of insects through spillage and to allow numbering the candy cups without adding the variable of weight of the numbering system used. After all insect groups were thoroughly dry, the candy cups were again weighed and insect biomass determined.

In a few cases, biomass was too great for the small candy cups; in which case, the group was placed in a larger, aluminum baking pan, then placed in the drying oven.

The emergence traps presented an additional problem because by the end of the study some of the traps had been in place for 56 weeks and production could not be expected to be the same as for a trap recently set. Therefore, to study biomass of emerging soil insects, fresh traps (5 in number) were placed over 5 m^2 of ground within the study site and left there throughout the month of October. Weekly collections of the material were made, and the insects were processed as with the other traps mentioned above.

SYSTEMATICS

The following arthropod orders (table 2, appendix) were encountered in Reserva Ducke, using the five trapping techniques. It is apparent that almost all terrestrial arthropod groups are represented, with the exception of parasitic orders such as Phthiraptera and Siphonaptera. These and other groups, such as Ricinuleida, Amblypygida, and Zoraptera, have been collected from Reserva Ducke, so that trapping techniques that were utilized are responsible for not finding these few groups during the study.

On four occasions during the study, 13 Dec. 1977, 25 April 1978, 12 Sept. 1978, and 3 Oct. 1978, all orders of arthropods were recorded. These results are demonstrated in tables 3 to 7 (see appendix) and graph 3. Identical light traps in the forest canopy at 15 m produced almost four times as many insects as at 1 m, of which 84–91% were Diptera.

Hymenoptera accounted for another 3 to 8%. Other groups were relatively insignificant. In the flight trap, Diptera and Hymenoptera were again the predominant groups, accounting for 79 and 11% of the total catch, respectively, with Coleoptera comprising another 2%. In emergence traps Diptera, Hymenoptera, and Collembola were the predominant groups, accounting for 35, 23, and 19% of the total number of individuals, respectively. Finally, in baited pitfall traps Diptera, Coleoptera, Acari, Collembola and Hymenoptera comprised 34, 25, 18, 13, and 9% of the attracted arthropods, respectively. Overall, it appears that Diptera and secondarily Hymenoptera are dominant groups, at least in terms of numbers (but see section on biomass). Surprisingly, the forest floor appeared to possess relatively little arthropod activity, and such groups as Acari and Collembola, which are generally considered to account for a large segment of arthropod activity, could only account for 21% of all arthropods collected from the emergence traps. However, where rich protein sources (baited pitfall traps) attracted arthropods from surrounding areas, these same two

ARTHROPODA   PRESENCE

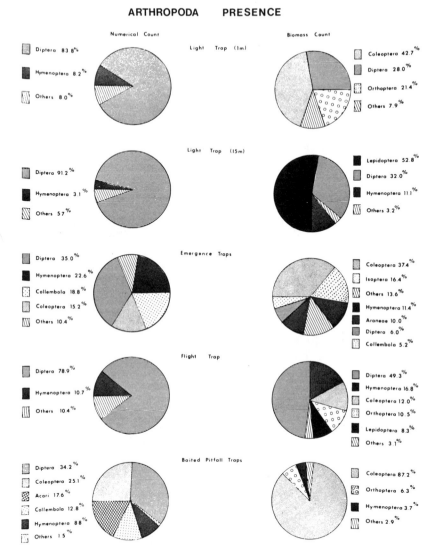

Graph 3.   Comparison of arthropod dominance in Reserva Ducke by numbers and biomass.

orders accounted for 30% of collected arthropods. The largest
insectan order, Coleoptera, was not predominant in terms of
individuals, but accounted for a far more significant portion of
the biomass, and richness was very high (see section on
Coleoptera).

December appeared to generally be the time of maximum population levels—as recorded by light, baited pitfall and emergence traps, although the flight trap indicates a much higher level of activity in April. As flight trap data between December and April are not directly comparable (because of the change in size of the trap), it might well be that use of the same flight trap over the whole time period would have resulted in indications of a December population peak.

CLASS: ONYCHOPHORA

Onychophorans (fig. 4) are an ancient group dating back to the Cambrian Period. Today, only two families exist: Peripatopsidae in humid areas of south temperate regions, and Peripatidae in equatorial zones of America, Africa, and Asia (Brinck 1956). Approximately 7 to 8 genera exist in each family, and around 70 species are presently known.

Onychophorans feed predominantly on animal food, but feed on some vegetable matter. Food is captured and defense secured by means of a stream of non-toxic, sticky fluid ejected from the oral papillae over a distance of up to 0.5 meter.

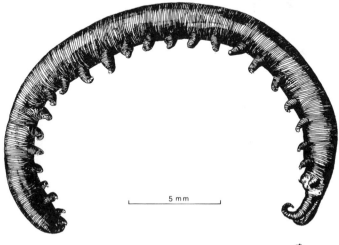

5 mm

Figure 4. Onychophora.

During the course of the study, only one onychophoran was collected—from the unbaited pitfall trap inside one of the emergence traps. This specimen was collected on 4 April, only one week after the trap was placed. The lack of other specimens indicates a quite low population level. Bührnheim (personal communication) indicates that onychophorans can be locally common on palms in the Belém area. It also appears that onychophorans form colonies, as most collections in the Amazon Basin indicate many individuals grouped together.

CLASS: ARACHNIDA

ORDER: SCORPIONIDA

Scorpionida is a primitive order of arachnids immediately distinguished by their long, recurved abdomen with terminal sting and large, heavily sclerotized pedipalps (fig. 5). They are nocturnal hunters, feeding on other arthropods which they immobilize with their sting.

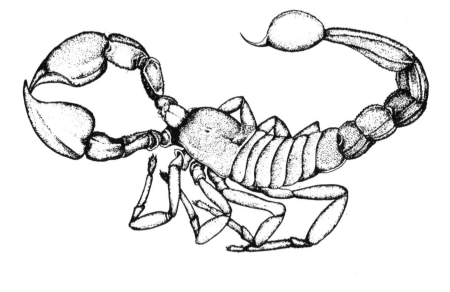

1 cm

Figure 5.   Scorpionida.

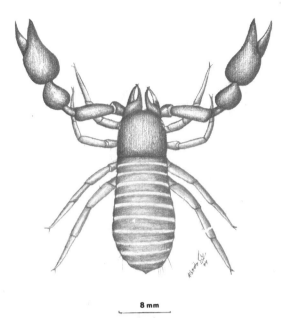

Figure 6.   Pseudoscorpionida.

A total of 53 scorpions were collected during the study, 41 of them from unbaited pitfall traps inside emergence traps and 12 from baited pitfall traps. Spatial distribution appears to have been "clumped," as 39 of the individuals were found in three emergence traps. There appeared to be little fluctuation in seasonal distribution, as these traps continued to collect scorpions for several months, with no synchronization between traps.

ORDER: PSEUDOSCORPIONIDA

Pseudoscorpions (fig. 6) are common inhabitants of the tropical forest floor, where they are predators on small, soft-bodied arthropods. They are also frequently encountered under tree bark and phoretically attached to bodies of large beetles. Mahnert (1979), in a recent study of Amazonian pseudoscorpions, lists 40 species from the Basin.

Pseudoscorpions were collected from both emergence traps and baited pitfall traps throughout the study. Although this order was not routinely monitored, their numbers present during the total counts indicate an average of 0.1 per baited pitfall

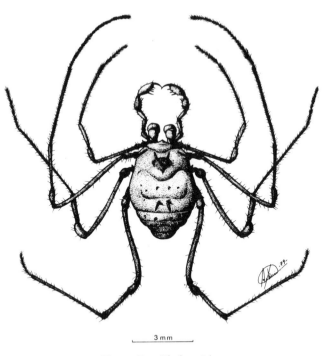

3 mm

Figure 7.   Phalangida.

trap and 0.2 per emergence trap. Many of those found in pitfall
traps were probably phoretic on larger beetles. Twelve specimens were sorted and sent to Dr. Volker Mahnert, Geneva,
Switzerland, who kindly identified them for us. They represent
five species, including one new genus and two new species.
The five species are: *Phymatochernes crassimanus* Mahnert, *Bra-
zilatemus browni* Muchmore, *Pseudochthonius homodentatus*
Chamberlin, *Lustrochernes similis* (Balzan), and *Tyrannochthonius*
(*T.*) *minor* Mahnert. Numbers and weight were small enough
to not register significantly in the biomass count.

ORDER: PHALANGIDA

Phalangida appear to be long-legged spiders (fig. 7), but are
immediately separable by the lack of a pedicel. These arachnids
can give off a disagreeable secretion when disturbed. They feed
on a wide variety of materials, from other arthropods to dead
organisms to plants.

Harvestmen, or granddaddy longlegs, were collected occasionally during the study in emergence traps. Their numbers
were not monitored, and biomass was too small to register.

ORDER: ACARI

Acari, or mites and ticks, are generally very small, diverse arachnids (fig. 8) which are adapted to many ecological niches.
The group is a very large one, but only recently received much
attention from taxonomists and ecologists, so that the exact
number of Acari can still only be guessed at. Largest and best-
known of the acarines are ticks. Other groups of mites live in
the soil, in hair follicles, on feathers, on plants, in the water,
etc.

Mites were noted in all types of traps, except light traps at
15 m. Those caught in the 1 m light traps were probably phoretic on insects. They represented 17.6% of arthropods pre-

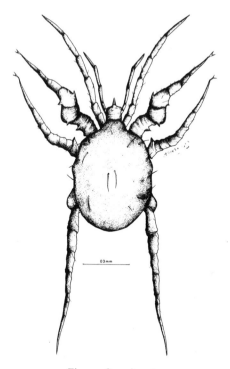

Figure 8. Acari.

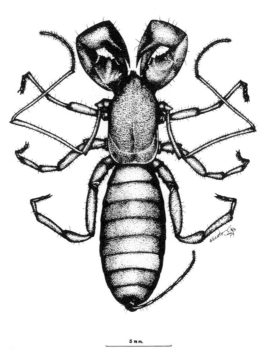

Figure 9.   Thelyphonida.

sent in baited pitfall traps, but only 0.6% of total arthropod
biomass in the same traps. The results of baited pitfall traps
(17.6%) are very similar to what other researchers have found
for the forest soil fauna in general. Beebe (1916) found 14% of
soil fauna to be mites at Belém and Williams (1941) found
24–25% to be mites in Panama. These results are in striking
contrast to Beck (1971) who found 70% of all soil fauna to be
mites near Manaus. The low number of mites in emergence
traps cannot be readily explained, except that these traps included small plants, fallen twigs, etc., and the numbers of associated insects (such as Scolytidae) were included in emergence
trap percentages.

ORDER: THELYPHONIDA

Thelyphonida, or whip scorpions (fig. 9), is a small group of
about 100 species living in tropical and subtropical areas of the
world. They range in size from about 1.5 to 13 cm. Whip

scorpions usually are ground dwellers, where they forage among detritus for soft-bodied insects. They defend themselves by means of abdominal glands which can emit formic or acetic acid.

Whip scorpions were occasionally encountered in emergence and baited pitfall traps, but numbers and biomass were too small to be significant. In all, 26 individuals were collected: 10 in emergence traps and 16 in baited pitfall traps. They were found in low numbers in almost all months, without any significant seasonal trend being noted.

ORDER: RICINULEIDA

Ricinuleida (fig. 10) is a rare order of arachnids living in humid tropical and subtropical regions of the world. Only about 25 species of Ricinuleida are known: 15 of them are from the New

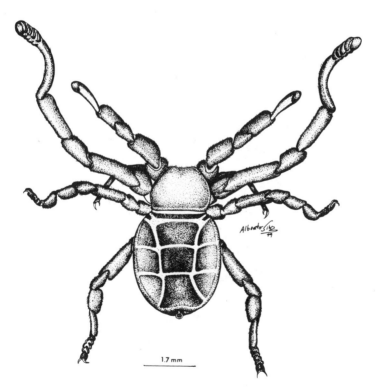

Figure 10. *Cryptocellus foedus* Westwood, Ricinuleida.

World, and all these in the genus *Cryptocellus*. They seem to
be most often found in caves, although they can be collected
on the forest floor in Amazonia.

   Although this order of Arachnida has at times been recorded
from Reserva Ducke, their population levels are always low
and none were encountered during this study. All collected
specimens from Reserva Ducke pertain to the species *Cryptocellus foedus* Westwood (for fuller discussion of this species, see
Beck and Schubart 1968).

ORDER: ARANEIDA

Araneida, or spiders (fig. 11), are a common, easily recognized
group of arachnids which live in a wide variety of habitats,
from silken balloons for sailing through the air, to freshwater,
to silken webs for capturing winged prey, to ground hunting
wolf spiders and tarantulas. Bates (1962) even recorded them

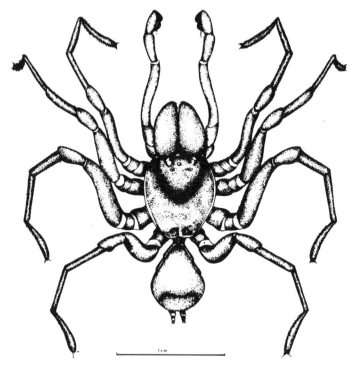

Figure 11.   Araneida.

capturing small birds in Amazonia. The group is very large, with about 40 families known from North America alone.

Spiders were an important component of the tropical forest fauna, being found in all types of traps. In terms of numbers, spiders represented 1.0% of 1 m light traps, 1.9% of emergence traps, and 0.2% of baited pitfall traps. In terms of biomass, spiders were insignificant, except in emergence traps, where they accounted for a full 10% of the biomass. The biomass study indicates that spiders in the 1 m light traps and baited pitfall traps were quite small, although from emergence trap data we realize that fairly heavy spiders are present in significant numbers. Thus, they must have actively avoided baited pitfall traps, or been too large for the mouth of the collecting bottles. No data is available on seasonal fluctuations in population levels.

ORDER: AMBLYPYGIDA
Amblypygida, or tailless whip scorpions, are large long-legged arachnids (fig. 12). In Amazonia they are nocturnal, forest predators often found clinging to hollow tree trunks. They move very rapidly and are difficult to capture.

The tailless whip scorpions have been collected infrequently at Reserva Ducke, but none were found in our traps. (For more details of Amblypygida from Reserva Ducke, see inside cover of *Acta Amazonica* 8(4) and Beck 1968).

CLASS: CRUSTACEA

While Arachnida and Insecta have evolved into some of the most abundant terrestrial animals, salt and freshwater have been dominated by the Crustacea. Many forms, such as crabs, shrimp, lobsters, and crawfish are familiar to most everyone. Less obvious, but equally important are the copepods which form a large component of the aquatic food chain, in the form of zooplankton.

Crustaceans are normally aquatic, but a few forms have adapted to parasitic or terrestrial life. Of these, only one order— Isopoda—was collected during our Reserva Ducke study. However, numbers were not monitored.

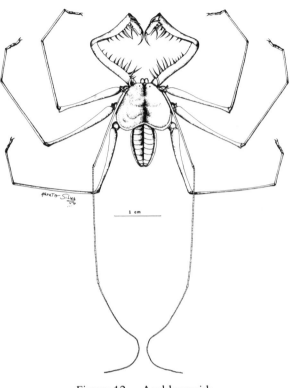

Figure 12.   Amblypygida.

ORDER: ISOPODA

Isopoda are mainly marine arthropods, but some groups can be found living in moist terrestrial habitats, such as under logs, rocks, or in damp cellars. They feed on vegetable matter, and a few species have become important pests of cultivated plants.

In Reserva Ducke, sowbugs (fig. 13) were found in both emergence traps and baited pitfall traps, being occasionally abundant in the latter. However, average numbers were small and biomass was not significant. Populational fluctuations were not monitored.

CLASS: DIPLOPODA

Diplopoda, or millipedes, are elongate, cylindrical arthropods who bear a large number of legs (fig. 14). Each body segment

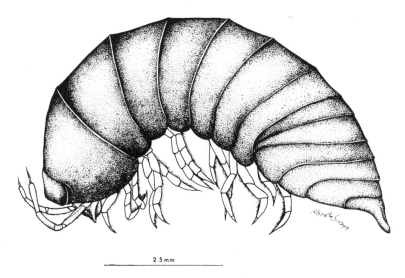

2.5 mm

Figure 13.   Isopoda.

appears to bear two pairs of legs, which gives rise to the name Diplopoda. Millipedes are usually common in moist areas where they scavenge the forest floor for plant material. Some species attack living plants, and have become agricultural pests. A few species are predaceous. When attacked, millipedes roll up into a ball with appendages withdrawn, and some species can give off a small amount of hydrogen cyanide gas. However, almost invariably millipedes are harmless to man.

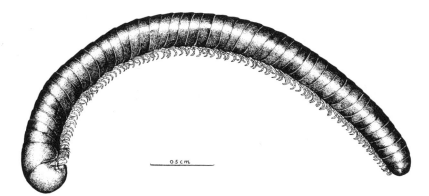

0.5 cm

Figure 14.   Diplopoda.

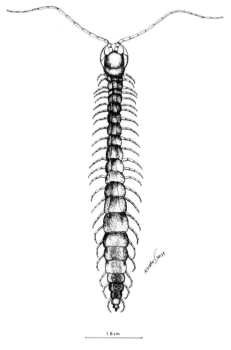

Figure 15.   Chilopoda.

Millipedes were occasionally collected from emergence and baited pitfall traps. Their numbers were low and biomass was too light to be significant.

CLASS: CHILOPODA

Chilopoda, or centipedes, are elongate, flattened, fast-moving arthropods with many pairs of legs (fig. 15). The first pair is modified as a poison gland, giving rise to the name Chilopoda. They have long antennae of 12 or more segments. Centipedes are usually ground-dwelling predators of other soft-bodied arthropods. When disturbed, they can inflict a painful wound with their modified poison fangs.

Centipedes were occasionally collected from both emergence traps and baited pitfall traps. A few of these predaceous arthropods in the genus *Scolopendra* can reach 18 cm in length in Reserva Ducke, but generally numbers and biomass were too small to be significant. Seasonal populational fluctuations were not monitored.

CLASS: SYMPHYLA

Symphylans are small, elongate, white arthropods with 12 pairs of legs (fig. 16). They live in dark, moist habitats such as under rocks or tree bark where they feed on vegetable matter. A few species have become agricultural pests, feeding on planted seeds.

Only one symphylan was collected during the study. This individual was taken from the pitfall trap within an emergence trap on 6 June. This individual was collected two months after the trap had been set. The very low density of symphylans at Reserva Ducke is in striking contrast to seasonally inundated areas near Manaus, where Adis (1979a) found symphylans to be among the predominant groups of Arthropoda.

CLASS: INSECTA

Insects may perhaps be the dominant form of terrestrial animal life. They are everywhere, from plant to soil, to water, to the air, to the food we eat. Their richness and genetic flexibility have allowed them to adapt and even flourish in the presence of man and his modern agricultural practices. Nowhere is this great richness more apparent than in moist, tropical ecosystems. The number of species of most insect groups is still poorly known from moist, tropical areas, and each day brings new revelations. Reserva Ducke is no exception, and the entomo-logical discoveries made in this biological reserve are both nu-

0.7 mm

Figure 16. Symphyla.

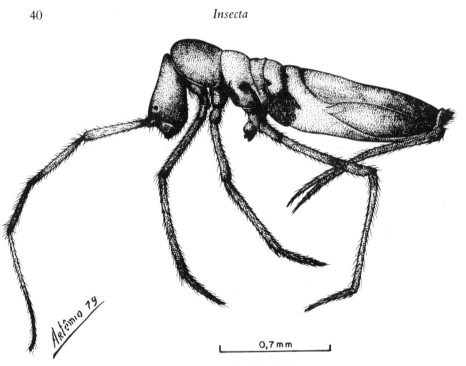

0,7 mm

Figure 17. Collembola.

merous and significant in terms of comprehensive studies of tropical forest ecosystems.

Insects made up the overwhelming bulk of the arthropods collected in Reserva Ducke. Between 82.2 and 99.9% of the individuals collected and 85.4 and 100% of the biomass were insects. All orders of insects have been found in Reserva Ducke, with the exception of Grylloblattodea and Raphidioptera, if these groups are considered to be orders. Our trapping techniques were not oriented toward collecting the wingless, parasitic orders Phthiraptera and Siphonaptera, and no Protura or Zoraptera were encountered during the study. All other hexapod orders were collected, in varying degrees of abundance.

ORDER: COLLEMBOLA

Collembolans, or spring-tails, are a very diverse group of usually very common, tiny, wingless insects bearing a ventral, forked appendage, by which means they are able to quickly "spring" several cm (fig. 17). Spring-tails are found in a wide variety of habitats from water surfaces to soil to snow, where they feed on a wide variety of materials from decaying plant matter to pollen, to feces, to fungi and many other materials. Mating is accomplished by males depositing spermathecae on the substrate, which are then picked up by the females.

In his index of Collembola, Salmon (1964) recorded 16 families and 386 genera worldwide.

Collembolans were found in all types of traps, except light traps at 15 m. That they were found in low numbers in light traps at 1 m probably indicates that they crawled into the trap by means of the support poles. In emergence traps and baited pitfall traps they represented 18.8 and 12.8% of arthropods collected, respectively. Because of their small size, collembolans only made up 5.2 and 0.2% of respective biomasses. Seasonal populational fluctuations were not monitored.

ORDER: DIPLURA

Diplurans are small, elongate, whitish insects with long antennae. They lack wings and eyes. They live in dark, moist areas, like under rocks and leaves, etc.

Two families of Diplurans, Campodeidae and Japygidae, were occasionally seen during the study. A total of only four diplurans were found in emergence traps and only one found in baited pitfall traps. Numbers and biomass were too small to be significant.

Family: Campodeidae

Campodeidae are easily recognized by their two, long, abdominal cerci (fig. 18). Campodeidae were collected only three times during 13 months, all from emergence traps. They were collected on 23 May, 6 June, and 20 June, indicating that possibly this time of year is strongly favored by campodeids for emergence, although the very low numbers prevent any definite conclusions being drawn.

Family: Japygidae

Japygidae differ from the previous family by modification of the abdominal cerci into stout, heavily sclerotized, pincer-like cerci.

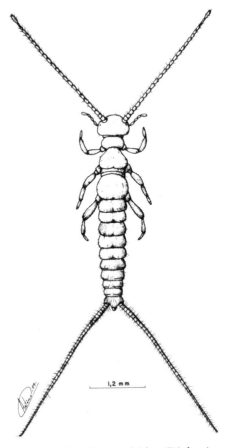

1,2 mm

Figure 18.   Campodeidae (Diplura).

Japygidae was encountered only twice to the study site, once in an emergence trap on 7 March, and once in a baited pitfall trap (fish and picric acid) on 4 April. Once again, an emergence is suggested (March-April) but low numbers prevent significance being concluded.

ORDER: MICROCORYPHIA (ARCHEOGNATHA)
Microcoryphia are primitive bristle-tails, bearing abdominal appendages on almost every segment and having only one mandibular articulation. They are elongate and flattened, wingless insects with three caudal abdominal filaments (fig. 19). Bodies are usually covered with scales. Brues et al. (1954) men-

ere collected at Reserva Ducke during the study, but from
total of only three individuals. All three were collected in a
/o week period from 21 Sept., until 3 Oct. 1978, from emerg-
ice traps and baited pitfall traps. Biomass was too small to
gister on our instruments.

Family: Ateluridae

teluridae are small, whitish, elongate-oval insects, tapering
udally, with three short, stout, abdominal appendages (fig.
).
This family is normally a subterranean associate of ant and
rmite nests (Watson 1970). Two individuals were found in
serva Ducke during the study, one in a baited pitfall trap
ces and chloral hydrate) on 27 Sept., and a second Atelurid
e week later in the pitfall trap inside an emergence trap.

Family: Nicoletiidae

icoletiidae are small, whitish, cylindrical insects with three,
1g, caudal filaments and long antennae (fig. 21). They are
bterranean dwellers, but not ant or termite commensals.
This family was collected only once, from an emergence trap
3 Oct. 1978. This is, as far as we know, the first published
ord of this family from Brazil.

ORDER: EPHEMEROPTERA

hemeroptera, or mayflies, are primitively winged insects
th two or four wings held rigidly laterally, or over the body.
vo extremely long, caudal filaments exist at the tip of the

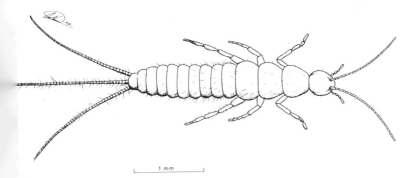

1 mm

Figure 20.   Ateluridae (Thysanura).

tioned only two families, Machilidae and
under the superfamily Machiloidea).

Only one family of this order, Meiner
during the 13 month study, in emergence
and baited pitfall traps. A total of 178
countered, including 27 in baited pitfall t
traps, and 127 in the flight trap. (Obv:
misnomer is this case, as the primitive l
sides of the trap). Generally, population l
at constant, low levels throughout the stu
inertellidae were trapped in the flight tra
27 Sept. 1978. No differences in attractanc
pitfall traps until the last two months of
1978), when 13 individuals were attrac
only 3 to traps baited with fish.

ORDER: THYSANU

Thysanura, or bristle-tails, are very sin
to the previous order, Microcoryphia,
in frequently not having segmental abdoi
having two mandibular articulations. Th
areas, such as many houses, where th
feeding on paper, book bindings and oth
Three families (Lepismatidae, Atelurid
have been enountered in Reserva Ducke

Two families of bristle-tails, Atelur

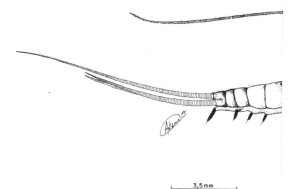

3,5 mm

Figure 19.   Meinertellidae (Micr

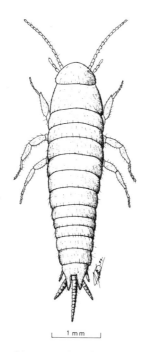

Figure 21.   Nicoletiidae (Thysanura).

abdomen (fig. 22). This is the only known group of insects in which immature insects bear functional wings, but shortly after emerging from the water, this last larval stage (subimago) sheds its skin, and an adult emerges. Adults may emerge in tremendous numbers at certain times of the year, causing traffic problems near rivers and lakes. These large numbers suggest their important role as a food for fishes in the aquatic ecosystem. However, perhaps the most notable aspect of mayflies is their short adult life span. After surviving several months to a year in the immature stage (naiad), adults may emerge and die within as little as 90 minutes, as with the white mayfly, *Ephoron album* (Edmonds et al. 1976). This gives rise to their name, Ephemeroptera.

Ephemeroptera is a medium-sized order, with 17 families and 68 genera known from North and Central America (Edmunds et al. 1976).

This order of aquatic insects was not studied, and only seen once, in a flight trap. This individual, in the family Baetidae, is discussed further in the section on unusual insects. Aquatic insects were occasionally collected, but the 500 m distance from Igarapé Barro Branco was apparently enough to almost completely eliminate Ephemeroptera from the study area.

ORDER: ODONATA

Odonata, or dragonflies and damselflies, are usually large insects with transparent, many-celled wings which do not fold. Eyes are large, and antennae tiny (fig. 23). They are in the air most of the daylight hours, capturing air-borne insects. Males have copulatory organs located at the base of the abdomen, where sperm are transferred to females from previously deposited sperm packets (spermatophores). Larvae are aquatic predators, feeding on aquatic insects, or occasionally larger prey.

Odonata is a medium-sized order, with 11 families and 423 species in North America, and about 5000 species world-wide (Borror et al., 1976). Because of the aquatic preference of Odonata, only four families were encountered during the study. They were encountered infrequently in the study traps, and always in the flight trap. One individual of Agrionidae was found on 18 April. Two specimens of Aeschnidae were taken

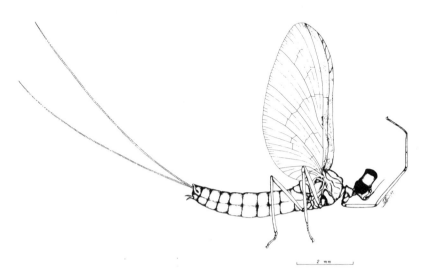

2 mm

Figure 22. *Baetodes* sp., Baetidae (Ephemeroptera).

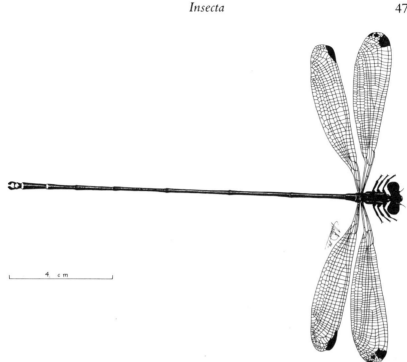

Figure 23.   Pseudostigmatidae (Odonata).

on 7 Feb. and 29 Aug. 1978. Coenagrionidae were collected on
21 Feb., 4 July, and 3 Oct. Finally, two individuals of Pseudostigmatidae were encountered on 2 May and 23 May. Although odonatans were not collected during the more than four
months from 3 Oct. until 6 Feb., the total collection of only
eight individuals does not allow us to make firm conclusions
from this seasonal data. Pseudostigmatids are known to live in
bromeliads, which are abundant at Reserva Ducke. The other
families may have come from stream habitats, at least 500 m
distance from the traps. These insects are all fairly strong fliers
and could disperse easily in this amiable environment.

The collected individuals did not provide enough biomass
to be of significance.

ORDER: ORTHOPTERA

Orthoptera includes a large number of well-known, medium-
sized to large-sized insects, such as crickets, grasshoppers, ka-

tydids, cockroaches, stick insects, and mantids. Immature
stages resemble wingless adults and development of wings is
external. Wings are generally long and narrow, with the forewing being more heavily sclerotized. Many groups have developed sound production for species and mate recognition.
Most groups are plant feeders or omnivorous, although a few
groups are predaceous. Some species have become very serious
agricultural pests, and a few of these pests are migratory. Many
means of defense are utilized in the Orthoptera, from camouflage coloration to strong development of leg spines and jumping ability, to secretion of chemicals, which in some cases can
be squirted more than a meter.

We have chosen to follow a classification in which five
Amazonian suborders are included in the Orthoptera. They are:
Caelifera, Blattoidea, Ensifera, Mantoidea, and Phasmoidea.
These groups were not monitored weekly, but total numerical
counts and biomass counts have given us a fairly good idea of
the abundance of Orthoptera in the tropical forest ecosystem.
Orthopterans were collected from all types of traps, and remarkably, all traps showed the same numerical abundance—
0.5%, with the exception that light trap catches revealed only
0.2% orthopterans. However, biomass counts perhaps give a
better idea of orthopteran impact on the ecosystem. In the light
traps at 1 m, 21% of biomass was orthopterans, while at 15 m
(which was only slightly less numerically—0.1%) 0.5% of biomass was orthopterans. This indicates the presence of more
heavily bodied orthopterans near the forest floor. Slightly over
10% of biomass of all insects collected in the flight trap were
orthopterans while only 3.8% of insect biomass emerging from
the soil were orthopterans. From baited pitfall traps, 6.3% of
collected insect biomass were orthopterans, but interestingly,
traps with feces and picric acid preservative showed only 0.5%
orthopterans, while all others showed 13.5–17.6% orthopterans. It is theorized that the large number of heavy scarab beetles
in feces–picric acid traps pushed the percentage of Orthoptera
biomass to its low level. Orthopterans accounted for 7.5% of
the arthropod biomass in all traps. It will be easily seen that the
influence, in terms of biomass, is greater near the forest floor,
where over 10% of the biomass of the flight trap was orthopterans and nearly one-quarter of those entering the 1 m light

trap. That only 3.8% of this biomass comes from emergence traps indicates that they are probably of greater importance in the lower vegetative strata.

SUBORDER: CAELIFERA

Caelifera, or short-horned grasshoppers, have short antennae and strongly developed hindlegs for jumping. Almost all species are plant feeders, sometimes increasing to tremendous numbers of individuals, who migrate in dense clouds over wide areas, devouring anything edible.

This suborder was seldom collected in any traps except the flight trap, where Orthoptera made up 10.5% of total biomass. Of this total, 54% was Acrididae (short-horned grasshoppers) while another 1.5% was Tetrigidae (pygmy grasshoppers).

SUBORDER: BLATTOIDEA

Blattoidea, or cockroaches and wood roaches, are medium to large sized, dorsally flattened insects with long antennae. They are best adapted for running, and are positively thigmotactic. They can occur in large numbers in domestic dwellings, where they feed on almost any starchy or proteinaceous substance, such as paper. They contaminate food, and in large numbers can leave an unpleasant odor. Tropical roaches are abundant in forests, where they are found on plants as well as on the ground, and are often brightly colored.

Cockroaches, along with the Gryllidae, formed the most conspicuous orthopteran components during the study. Blattoidea was found in all traps, and comprised the following orthopteran biomass: 53 to 74% of light traps, 33% of the flight trap, 10 to 53% of baited pitfall traps (depending on bait and preservative), and 49% of emergence traps.

SUBORDER: ENSIFERA

Ensifera, or crickets, katydids, mole crickets, and their relatives, are insects with long antennae and highly developed hindlegs for jumping (fig. 24). Mole crickets have become highly modified soil dwellers, with strong forelegs and shortened antennae. Sound production has become highly developed, and is generally accomplished by rubbing one wing over another. Most ensiferans are plant feeders, although some are predatory.

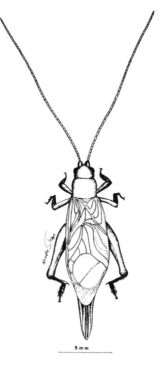

Figure 24. Gryllidae (Orthoptera).

In this suborder, Gryllidae (crickets) were found with all trapping methods. They included 26 to 47% of all orthopterans in light traps, 5% of the flight trap, 53–90% of baited pitfall traps, and 50% of emergence traps. Their presence was particularly noticable in the pitfall traps baited with fish, where crickets represented almost 10% of the total biomass of arthropods. The only other ensiferan family recorded was Tettigoniidae, which accounted for 5.2% of orthopteran biomass in the flight trap.

SUBORDER: MANTOIDEA

Mantoidea, or mantids, are large, predatory insects, whose most distinctive character is the large, raptorial forelegs they use for grasping and securing prey. Some tropical species have highly developed camouflage coloration, with expanded appendages resembling leaves or flowers.

Preying mantids were only occasionally encountered during

the study, and then only in the flight trap. They accounted for only 0.5% of orthopteran biomass in the flight trap and a negligible amount overall.

SUBORDER: PHASMOIDEA

Phasmoidea, or stick insects, usually have greatly elongated bodies and appendages, which closely resemble twigs of trees. Males and females are sometimes dimorphic with males being only ⅓ the size of females. Phasmids are large, plant feeders, who can occasionally cause extensive damage to ornamental plants. Many species are wingless, but winged forms fold short wings over the very narrow body.

This suborder, like the Mantoidea, was only collected occasionally in the flight trap where they represented a negligible amount of biomass, even among the orthopterans.

ORDER: DERMAPTERA

The Dermaptera, or earwigs, are elongate, flattened insects with long antennae, and large, pincer-like cerci (fig. 25). Forewings are short, sclerotized flaps. The hindwings are rounded, and fold under the forewing flaps when at rest. Earwigs are attracted to lights, and usually occur hidden on the ground under rocks, boards, etc. Most dermapterans are general scavengers, and some are plant feeders. A few species enter plant houses and cause damage to flowers. They are much more common in tropical than temperate climates.

Dermaptera were frequently collected in the Reserva Ducke traps, usually in the baited pitfall traps, and also occasionally in all others as well. A total of 4358 individuals were collected

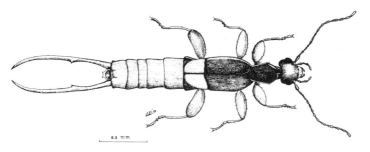

Figure 25.   Dermaptera.

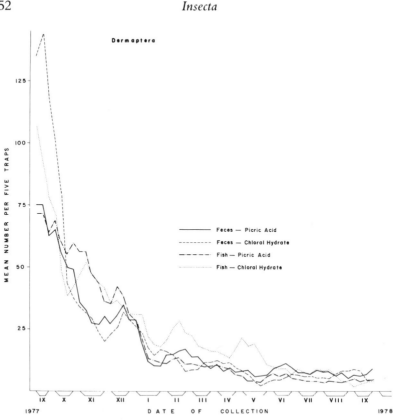

Graph 4.   Collections of Dermaptera from baited pitfall traps.

in baited pitfall traps between 6 Sept. 1977 and 3 Oct. 1978. There were no significant differences between fish and feces bait (P > .10), or between the two killing-preservative agents (P > .10). However, there was a very significant difference (P < .001) in catches throughout the season, with early catches being much larger than those later on (graph 4). For example, the period between 6 Sept. 1977 and 4 Oct. 1977, had captures of 1233 dermapterans, while during the same period of 1978 only 87 dermapterans were captured.

In emergence traps 55 earwigs were collected. Over half of this total were collections made during Sept.–Nov. 1977, from traps set in September and October. Although the baited pitfall traps demonstrate strong indications of a "trapping out" of earwig populations near the traps, the emergence trap data tend to support high population levels of earwigs on the forest floor during September—November 1977. The lack of a recurrence of this population peak in 1978 may just be due to strong yearly population oscillations.

Only 17 earwigs were caught in the flight trap, and these collections were sporadic throughout the year. Additionally, two dermapterans were collected in 1 m light traps, and five more in 15 m light traps. Biomass contribution of Dermaptera was negligible when the count was taken in October 1978.

ORDER: ISOPTERA

Isoptera, or termites, are small to medium-sized insects which live in colonies and feed primarily on wood (fig. 26). They have a well-developed caste system of reproductives and workers. At one time, frequently triggered by heavy rainfall, large numbers of winged reproductives will leave a nest for a mating

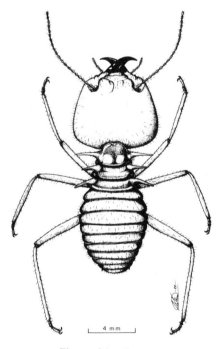

Figure 26. Isoptera.

flight. Single pairs will lose their wings (via pre–determined breakage points) and form a new colony. This pair becomes the king and queen of the new colony, and progeny develop the worker caste. When the colony is well established, other winged reproductives are produced. Some workers develop extremely large head and mandibles or a chemical spray structure on the head. These workers are called soldiers, and their task is defense of the colony. Workers, unlike ants, consist of individuals of both sexes.

Often times, nests are formed in the ground, but other species may form mound nests or even mud nests in trees. Mound nests are quite hard, and at times can be several meters high, creating a serious problem for agriculture. Termites are also infamous pests of wooden structures, feeding on the interior while leaving the surface intact, until the structure collapses. However, recent research indicates that termites play a far more beneficial role in tropical ecosystems, breaking down and recycling wood and animal feces, and fixing nitrogen in the soil.

Araujo (1977) recorded 7 families, 73 genera, and 499 species of termites from the New World, most of these from the Neotropical Region. Bandeira (1979) recorded 2 families and 15 genera in a central Amazonian primary forest.

Termites are a major component of tropical forest ecosystems, and were found in all types of Reserva Ducke traps. Their numbers were not monitored regularly, although occasionally very large numbers were encountered in the baited pitfall traps. During the four weeks in which total counts were kept, numbers of termites were proportionally insignificant. However, because of their relatively large size, winged reproductives accounted for more than 1% of arthropod biomass in the flight trap, and non–winged forms accounted for more than 16% of biomass in emergence traps.

ORDER: EMBIOPTERA

Embioptera, or web–spinners, are small to medium–sized insects, immediately distinguishable by their greatly expanded fore–tarsi (fig. 27). These tarsi contain a silk gland, from which silk is spun to form a covering on tree trunks or under rocks and fallen logs. Embiopterans feed on various plant materials, and when disturbed can rapidly move backwards.

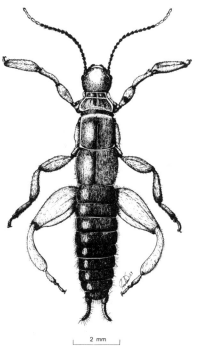

Figure 27. Embioptera.

The order is a medium-sized one, with Ross (1970) listing 14 families and about 800 species worldwide.

Web-spinners are much more common in tropical climates than in temperate ones, and a total of 116 individuals were collected from all traps, except baited pitfall traps. They were most abundant in emergence traps, where 66 were encountered. They appeared to be present at all times of the year in about equal frequency (graph 5). There were about twice as many web-spinners collected in light traps at 15 m as in the same traps at 1 m height. Relative numbers and biomass were always too low to be significant when compared to other arthropod groups.

ORDER: PLECOPTERA

Plecoptera, or stoneflies, are medium to large-sized, dorsally flattened insects with long antennae and cerci. The prothorax

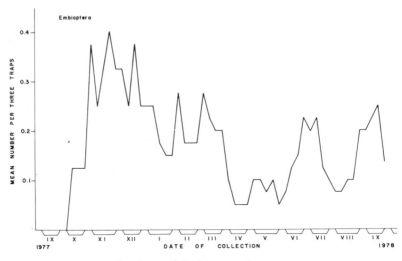

Graph 5.   Collections of Embioptera from emergence traps.

is quadrate, and wings are held flat over the body (fig. 28).
Immature stages are aquatic, where they scavange for plant
matter, or are occasionally predaceous. Adults usually do not
feed, and are usually encountered near water.

Stoneflies are known from only one family, Perlidae, in the
Amazon Basin. Despite the distance the study site was located
from any major streams, one individual was taken from the
flight trap on 25 July 1978.

ORDER: PSOCOPTERA

Psocoptera, or wood lice, are small, large-headed insects with
long antennae and reduced wing venation (fig. 29). They are
often encountered in books, under bark, or in other dark areas,
where they feed on mold, fungi, pollen, and dead insects. They
can be a serious problem in tropical insect collections.

Wood lice were well represented at the study site, with 2144
individuals being collected, using all trapping techniques. The
density was quite large, with 20 families recorded. All trapping
techniques were effective collectors, except baited pitfall traps,
where only 13 individuals were found (graphs 6, 7, 8). The
occurence of Psocoptera in baited pitfall traps was probably
fortuitous. More than twice as many psocopterans were col-

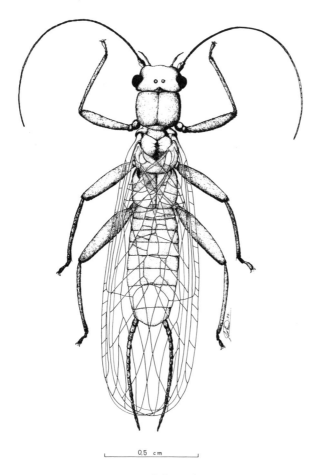

0,5 cm

Figure 28.   Perlidae (Plecoptera).

Graph 6.   Collections of Psocoptera from 1 and 15 m light traps.

Insecta

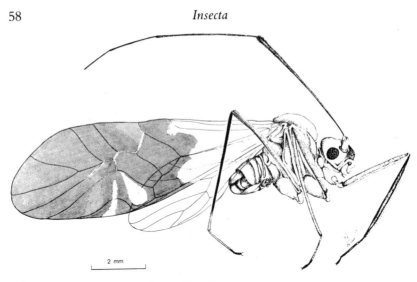

Figure 29.   Psocoptera.

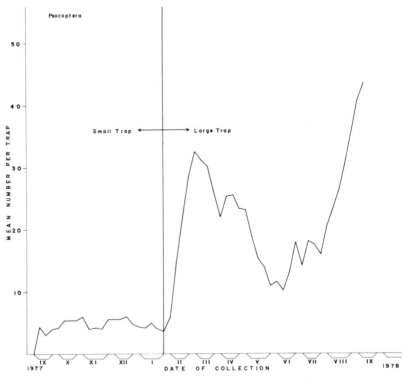

Graph 7.   Collections of Psocoptera from the flight trap.

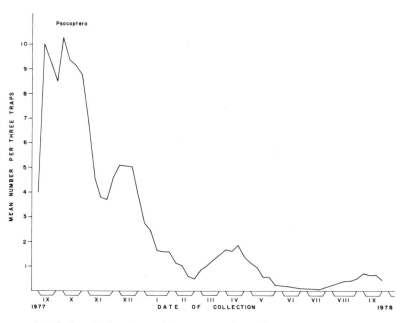

Graph 8. Collections of Psocoptera from the emergence traps.

lected at 15 m in the canopy, as near ground level at 1 m (523 and 242 specimens, respectively). This probably reflects greater canopy activity where foliage surface is greater. However, 437 wood lice were taken from emergence traps, indicating that litter activity was also high. But, the largest number of individuals (929) were taken from the flight trap, indicating high mobility of psocopterans at this site. With respect to other arthropod groups, Psocoptera never attained high enough population levels to be comparatively significant, either in terms of numbers or biomass. Seasonally, light trap records seem to indicate a population peak in early December, while flight trap records were highest in September. Possibly, populations rise in December, but maximal dispersal doesn't take place until September.

ORDER: THYSANOPTERA
Thysanoptera, or thrips, are very small insects, immediately recognizable by their feathery fore- and hindwings (fig. 30). Development of nymphs includes some development of internal

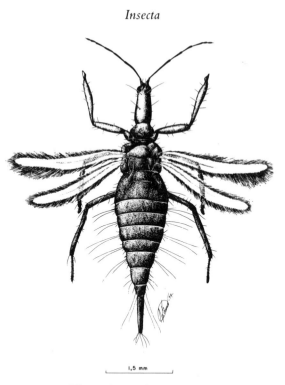

1,5 mm

Figure 30.   Thysanoptera.

wings and a last, non-feeding instar, which makes them inter-
mediate between insects with complete and incomplete meta-
morphosis. Most thrips are plant feeders, where they can cause
damage when populations are high. Other thrips are predaceous, feeding on other soft-bodied insects, especially other
thrips.

Thrips were not monitored during the study, but were more
or less regularly encountered in all traps, where they averaged
0.5 per trap, and baited pitfall traps where they averaged 0.2
per trap. The small size of these insects prevented their regis-
tering significantly in the biomass count. It appears, from comparison of total counts in emergence traps, that they were more
abundant in December than in April, September, or October.

ORDER: HEMIPTERA

Hemiptera, or true bugs, are a large assemblage of rather diverse
insects. All have sucking mouthparts and incomplete meta-

morphosis. Most are plant-feeders, and some are considered among our most important agricultural pests. A few families are predatory, and some reduviids are vectors of human diseases. The two suborders are quite distinct, with Heteroptera usually having the basal part of the forewing (tegmen) heavily sclerotized while the apical part is membranous. In the suborder Homoptera, forewings are completely membranous.

We are following the recent views of Woodward et al. (1970) and others in placing Heteroptera and Homoptera together as suborders of a single order Hemiptera, although a considerable number of specialists consider them as two distinct orders.

This order was well represented in our samples, with a total of 16 families of Heteroptera and 21 families of Homoptera being found during the study. They are often cited as vectors of plant diseases, and yet very little is known about them in the Amazon region. With further agricultural development in this area, some of these hemipterans will undoubtedly become very important economically, as has already happened with pasture spittle-bugs (Cercopidae).

Hemipterans were found in all traps, where they comprised 1.8% of the arthropods in 1 m light traps, 0.8% of arthropods in the 15 m light traps, 1.2% in emergence traps, 1.2% in the flight trap and 0.3% in baited pitfall traps. In terms of biomass, Hemiptera made up 0.5% of arthropods in the 1 m light traps, 0.3% in the 15 m light traps, 3.7% in emergence traps, 1.5% in the flight trap, and 0.2% in the baited pitfall traps (graph 3).

A total of 10,928 hemipterans were collected during the study, with Cicadellidae (21%), Schizopteridae (18%), Derbidae (17%), and Cixiidae (12%) being the predominant families. The family Achilixiidae is recorded for the first time from Brazil.

Family: Acanalonidae

Acanalonidae is a family of planthoppers having wings held roof-like over the body. They are usually green with rounded wings. They superficially resemble Flatidae, but have few costal crossveins and no protuberances along the costal vein. Fennah (1954) placed Acanalonidae as a subfamily of Issidae, but few other authors have accepted this classification. Acanalonidae is a small family, with Metcalf (1954a) listing 13 genera and 81 species worldwide. Of these, 72 species are found in the Western Hemisphere.

Only one specimen of Acanalonidae was encountered during the study, in a 15 m light trap on 27 Sept. 1978. This family has not been frequently collected in the central Amazon Basin, and the low number caught during the study is to be expected.

Family: Achilidae

Achilidae is a family of planthoppers generally recognized by the "open" clavus and overlapping apices of the forewings. They are generally small, and many of them are dorso-ventrally flattened, although a large number of Amazonian individuals in the genus *Sevia* are laterally flattened. They feed on plant fluids, and are frequently encountered on tree trunks. Nymphs are believed to feed on fungi (O'Brien 1971).

This family is still known from only 26 species in all of South America, but during the study we found achilids to be both common and diverse. They constituted almost 3% of all hom-opterans caught, and were captured from all types of traps, except baited pitfall traps. In all, 322 achilids were collected, with over three times as many being captured in 15 m light traps as 1 m light traps. Flight trap data indicate a rather consistent, low-level presence of this family throughout the year. Emergence trap data appear to show the same trend, although numbers were somewhat higher during November and December (graphs 9, 10, 11).

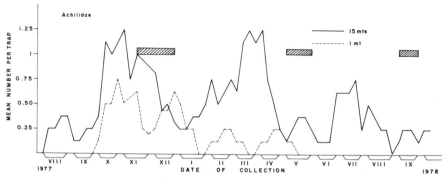

Graph 9.   Collections of Achilidae (Hemiptera) from 1 and 15 m light traps.

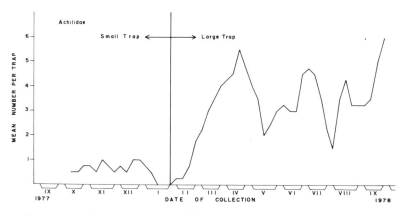

Graph 10.   Collections of Achilidae (Hemiptera) from the flight trap.

Family: Achilixiidae

Achilixiidae is the smallest family of planthoppers, with only 12 known species from the Neotropical Region and the Philippines. They are small, laterally flattened insects with a very characteristic lateral protuberance on the second abdominal segment. Some Cixiidae also have a lateral protuberance, but the protuberance is always double in Cixiidae, and they have a "closed" claval vein, while in Achilixiidae this vein is "open." Achilixiids are not commonly encountered in other areas, but are fairly abundant in the Amazon Basin. They were commonly collected in our traps, especially the flight trap, where they accounted for 2.5% of all hemipterans. These are the first records of this family from Brazil. Flight trap data (graph 12) indicate two possible population peaks, one during April, and the other in Aug.–Sept.

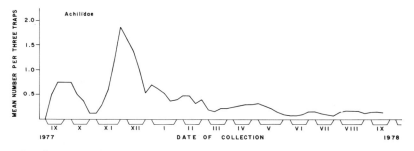

Graph 11.   Collections of Achilidae (Hemiptera) from emergence traps.

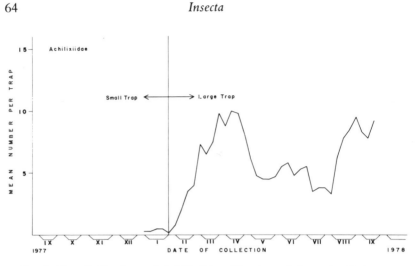

Graph 12.   Collections of Achilixiidae (Hemiptera) from the flight trap.

Family: Aethalionidae

Aethalionidae are small to medium-sized insects with protruding eyes. Their systematic position is still not clear. Some authorities consider them as Cicadellidae (without a row of tibial spines), while the majority of specialists consider them Membracidae (treehoppers) without the posteriorly extended pronotum.

This family, consisting of 8 genera and only 47 species, is confined to the Oriental and Neotropical Regions. Only four aethalionids were collected during the study, three from the flight trap on 7 March, 21 March, and 30 May. One additional individual was found in a 15 m light trap on 13 Sept.

Family: Aleyrodidae

Aleyrodidae, or whiteflies, are very small insects which are normally covered by a powdery, white wax. They can occur in large numbers in protected areas, where they cause plant yellowing from their feeding on the sap. Nymphs are rounded and scale-like. Bondar (1923) listed 3 subfamilies, 23 genera, and 80 species from Brazil.

Aleyrodidae were commonly collected in 15 m light traps, but only rarely in 1 m light traps and the flight trap. Light trap records indicate a rather constant, low population level throughout the year.

Family: Cercopidae

Cercopidae, or spittlebugs, are small to medium-sized, jumping insects. Larvae form a small, foamy nest on a plant, in which they live, feeding on the plant sap. Sometimes they will feed on above-ground roots. Many are brightly colored, with red, orange, and yellow predominating. Some species are serious pests of pastures and sugar cane.

Cercopidae have become increasingly important in the Amazon Basin in recent years with the advent of large pasturage areas, which have been widely destroyed by these insects, especially *Deois incompleta* (Walker). In the Manaus area, approximately 60 species have been encountered, of which only three are to be found in open grasslands. Most are inhabitants of primary forests where many were seen feeding on the mat of plant roots at the soil surface, and most were collected from emergence traps. Spittlebugs were found in the traps at all times, and no seasonal peak was indicated (graph 13).

Family: Cicadellidae

Cicadellidae, or leafhoppers, are small to medium-sized homopterans easily recognized by the row of spines they bear on the hind tibia. Some are brightly colored or boldly patterned. These insects quickly jump when disturbed. Leafhopper nymphs and adults feed on plant fluids and in large numbers can cause

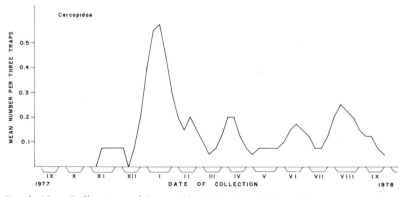

Graph 13.   Collections of Cercopidae (Hemiptera) from the emergence traps.

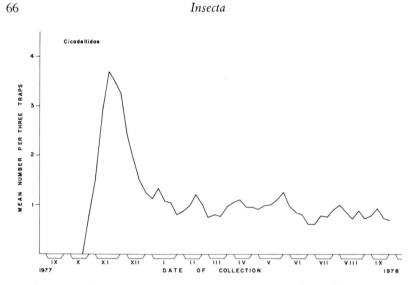

Graph 14.   Collections of Cicadellidae (Hemiptera) from the emergence
traps.

economic damage. Some species are also known to be vectors
of plant viral diseases.

Cicadellidae is a very large and abundant family. They are
found in most terrestrial habitats, but seem to reach maximum
density in grasslands. At times, lights can attract vast quantities
at one time.

Cicadellids were the most commonly encountered family of
Hemiptera in Reserva Ducke, although they did not reach the
tremendous numbers often seen in grasslands. A total of 2318
leafhoppers were collected, of which more than half were from
the flight trap. Emergence trap data seem to indicate a population peak from Sept. to Nov. (graph 14). Flight trap data are
a little more difficult to evaluate, because of the two sized traps
used during the study, but by October when the study ended,
the population of leafhoppers had risen to a 8-month high level
(graph 16). Collections from the light traps at 15 m height
indicate largest catches in December, March, and June–July
(graph 15).

Family: Cicadidae

Cicadidae, or cicadas, are large homopterans with three dorsal
ocelli. Wings are normally transparent, but some tropical spe-

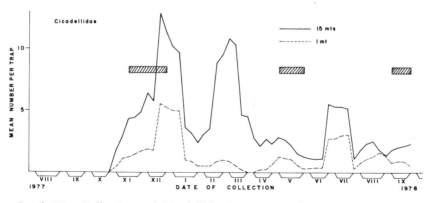

Graph 15. Collections of Cicadellidae (Hemiptera) from 1 and 15 m light
traps.

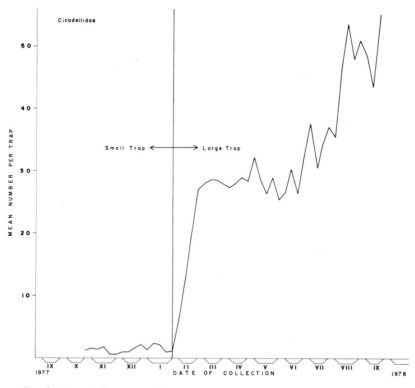

Graph 16. Collections of Cicadellidae (Hemiptera) in the flight trap.

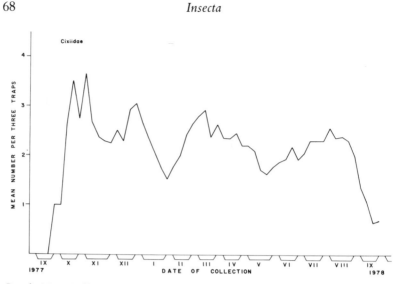

Graph 17.   Collections of Cixiidae (Hemiptera) from the emergence traps.

cies have brightly colored wings. This family is fairly large. Metcalf (1963) recorded 131 genera and 1162 species worldwide.

Cicadas are conspicuous inhabitants of tropical forest ecosystems, where at certain times of the year their calls can be deafening. Nymphs feed on tree roots, and at emergence some species form a conspicuous mud tube above the soil surface. However, during the study only one cicada was captured, emerging into a soil eclector on 21 March.

Family: Cixiidae

Cixiidae are small, laterally compressed planthoppers that are generally black and white or brown and white in coloration. They have a "closed" clavus, and usually small expansions along the wing veins, giving the veins a beaded appearance. Metcalf (1936) recorded 786 species in this family.

Cixiidae was one of the most commonly encountered families (graphs 17, 18) of Hemiptera in Reserva Ducke. Feeding on plant roots as immatures and actively attracted to light as adults, these insects were collected from all types of traps, and accounted for more than 12% of all Hemipterans in the traps. Data from the flight trap indicates an adult population peak in late August and early September.

Family: Delphacidae

Delphacidae are small planthoppers with a characteristic, large, moveable spur on each hind tibia. This is the largest family of planthoppers, with Metcalf (1943) recording 137 genera and 1114 species worldwide.

Delphacidae are common inhabitants of grasslands where they are known vectors of plant diseases of sugar cane, corn, etc. They are less frequently encountered in forest ecosystems, but still a total of 109 were captured during the study, from all types of traps, except baited pitfall traps. Numbers were highest in the emergence traps (graph 19), where 76 were recorded.

Family: Derbidae

Derbidae are laterally compressed, small to medium-sized plan-thoppers with short terminal rostral segment. Adults and nymphs feed on fungus and are often encountered on tree trunks or the underside of leaves. The group is a fairly large one, with 111 genera and 733 species recorded (Metcalf 1945).

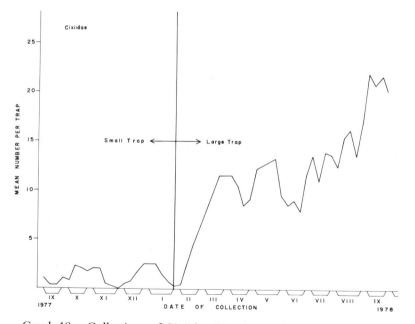

Graph 18.   Collections of Cixiidae (Hemiptera) from the flight trap.

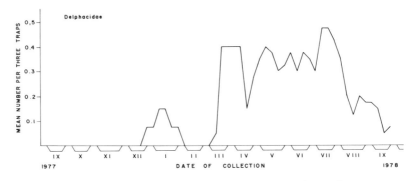

Graph 19.   Collections of Delphacidae (Hemiptera) from the emergence
            traps.

Derbidae was the third most common family of Hemiptera
at the Reserva Ducke study site. They accounted for almost
18% of all hemipterans. A total of 1927 individuals were collected from all types of traps, although only one from baited
pitfall traps. Both light trap heights indicated a peak emergence
of adults in Nov.–Jan., but the peak at 15 m came approximately three weeks before the peak at 1 m (graph 20). Biomass
of Derbidae was too low to be significant.

Family: Dictyopharidae
Dictyopharidae are medium-sized to large, elongate planthoppers distinguished by a long pre-cephalic protuberance. Almost
all are green or brown in color. Most temperate species live on
grasses, but many tropical species are forest dwellers. Metcalf
(1957) recorded 119 genera and 489 species worldwide.

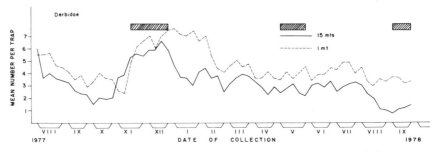

Graph 20.   Collections of Derbidae (Hemiptera) from 1 and 15 m light traps.

Few individuals of Dictyopharidae were encountered in the traps, but two of the species caught are among the largest of the family, *Lappida longirostris* Schmidt (fig. 31) and *Plegmaptera prasina* Spinola. Almost all dictyopharids were caught in the flight trap, although 3 were caught in light traps, both at 1 m and 15 m. Ten of the 12 dictyopharids in the flight trap were caught during the months of August, September, and October.

Family: Flatidae

Flatidae are laterally flattened, medium-sized planthoppers with small protuberances along the claval vein and a large number of crossveins, including the costal region. Nymphs and adults often live communally on trees, vines or herbaceous vegetation. Some tropical species are brightly colored and can be easily mistaken for moths. Metcalf (1957) recorded 212 genera and 981 species.

A total of 28 flatids were caught during the study, all from light and flight traps. No seasonal trend was detected from the low numbers encountered, but they were collected in almost all months of the year.

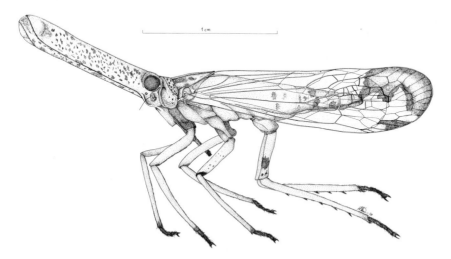

Figure 31.   *Lappida longirostris* Schmidt, Dictyopharidae (Hemiptera).

Family: Fulgoridae

Fulgoridae are medium-sized to very large planthoppers distinguished by the reticulate crossveins of the tegmen. Most species live on tree trunks and have rather dull-colored tegmina, but brightly colored hindwings. On the wing, they look like butterflies. Some species have elongate, hollow protuberances in front of the head, and in one Amazonian species this takes the form of a many-toothed, saw-like structure.

In Amazonia, the family is commonly collected, but never in large quantities. Metcalf (1947) recorded 108 genera and 543 species worldwide. Approximately 60 species have been collected from the Manaus area, but only two fulgorids were taken during the study. These two individuals were taken in the flight trap on April 18 and May 9.

Family: Issidae

Issidae are usually medium-sized, rather stout, almost rounded planthoppers. Most are pale to dark brown in coloration. Issids are most common in open grasslands, where they feed on grass stems. Metcalf (1958) recorded 206 genera and 981 species worldwide.

Twenty-four were collected during the study, and all but one of these were found in the flight trap. Numbers were too low to indicate any definite populational emergence peaks, but the family appeared to be present in the adult stage throughout the year.

Family: Lophopidae

Lophopids are medium-sized, clear winged planthoppers, which appear similar to Cixiidae, but have a very small second tarsal segment.

Lophopidae is one of the smallest families in the Fulgoroidea, with only 4 genera and 6 species known from South America (Metcalf 1955). What little is known of the life cycle indicates that they are plant-sap feeders. During the study in Reserva Ducke one individual was collected in the flight trap on 5 Sept. 1978.

Family: Membracidae

Membracidae, or treehoppers, are small to medium-sized insects which are immediately distinguished from other homopterans by the caudal projections of the pronotum. In some Amazonian species this can take the form of elaborately bifurcated and bulbously expanded structures. Membracidae is a large family, with Metcalf and Wade (1965) recording 307 genera and 2298 species.

Treehoppers are among the more common groups of insects in tropical forest ecotome habitats, where they feed on plant sap. They are usually tended by ants which are a distinctive indicator of membracid presence. They are not so easily found deep within the forest, and only 18 were found in the traps, of which 17 were in the flight trap. They appeared to be present as adults in low populational levels throughout the year.

Family: Monophlebiidae (*Margarodidae*)

Monophlebiidae, or giant coccids, are a small group of rather large scale insects. Females form large, rounded scales on plant roots or stems, which in some species can be used as shellac or as ornamental jewelry. Males are much less frequently encountered, and have long antennae and only one pair of wings, the hind ones.

Monophlebiidae are seldom collected with traps, because only adult males and first instar nymphs are mobile. However, one adult male was taken from the flight trap on 8 Aug. 1978.

Family: Nogodinidae

Nogodinidae are medium-sized planthoppers, that are laterally or dorso-ventrally flattened. Many have striking black and white or green color patterns, thus giving the appearance of small butterflies. They feed on plant sap, often of forest understory bushes and shrubs, or grass stems of savannahs.

Nogodinidae is another of the smaller fulgorid families, with only eight genera and 28 species recorded in Metcalf's (1954b) catalogue from South America. Kramer (1976) has since added seven new species and reduced the status of three others in *Bladina*. Only nine individuals were collected during the study,

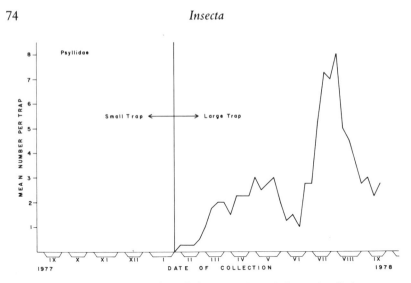

Graph 21.   Collections of Psyllidae (Hemiptera) from the flight trap.

all in the flight trap. Six of the nogodinids were found between
April 12 and May 23.

Family: Psyllidae

Psyllidae, or jumping plant lice, are small, robust homopterans
with long antennae and jumping legs. They live on plant sap
as both nymphs and adults. This group is fairly large and contains a number of plant pest species. Some species form numerous leaf galls on a plant, and other species can transmit plant
viral diseases.

One hundred psyllids were found during the study, of which
95 were in the flight trap. There appeared to be a population
peak at about 18 July, but some psyllids were collected throughout the year (graph 21).

Family: Tropiduchidae

This small family of small to medium-sized planthoppers have
a characteristic band of crossveins across the tegmen.

Tropiduchidae is known from only 13 genera and 27 species
in continental South America. They feed on plant fluids. During
the study only three individuals were encountered, one in a 15
m light trap on 27 Sept. 1977, and the other two in the flight

trap on 25 Oct. 1977, and 6 Sept. 1978. A Sept.–Oct. flight
period may be indicated.

Family: Alydidae

Alydidae, or broad-headed bugs, are medium-sized, elongate
heteropterans with heads as wide as the pronotum. Broad-
headed bugs are plant feeders and frequently collected sweeping
in grassy areas. At Reserva Ducke, only two individuals were
found, one in a 15 m light trap on 13 Sept. 1977, and the other
in the flight trap on 4 July 1978.

Family: Anthocoridae

Anthocoridae, or minute pirate bugs, are small predaceous insects feeding on other insects, but occasionally biting man and
causing painful irritation. They accounted for almost 5% of
hemipterans collected in the baited pitfall traps, and were found
in smaller numbers in light traps and the emergence traps (graph
22). In the pitfall traps, numbers were highest in Sept. 1977,
diminishing to very low levels by June 1978, and then beginning
to rise again in Sept. 1978. There was no statistically significant
preference for fish/feces ($.10 > P > .05$) or picric acid/chloral
hydrate ($.25 > P > .10$).

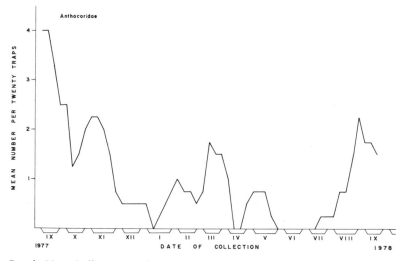

Graph 22.   Collections of Anthocoridae (Hemiptera) from baited pitfall
traps.

Family: Aradidae

Aradidae, or flat bugs, are as the common name indicates, very flattened and usually a mottled brown or black in color. They rest on tree bark, taking plant fluids while remaining inactive and well-camouflaged. Only three aradids were captured during the study, one in the flight trap on 20 Feb. and the other two in emergence traps on 24 Jan. and 7 March.

Family: Cydnidae

Cydnidae, or burrower bugs, are rounded, black bugs with characteristic spiny hindlegs. Most cydnids feed on roots and other underground parts of plants, while one genus, *Sehirus*, feeds on above ground stems and leaves. In the most recent revision of the family, Froeschner (1960) treated 141 species in 15 genera from the New World.

Cydnidae was one of the most commonly encountered heteropteran families during the study. Burrower bugs were frequently collected from baited pitfall traps, where they accounted for 22% of all Hemiptera.

Seasonally, cydnids appeared to be attracted to baited pitfall traps during the months of September–October (graph 23) and were much more common in traps baited with feces as opposed to fish (graph 24), and traps using chloral hydrate as opposed to picric acid preservative (graph 25). In each case, the probability is less than .001 that the baits and preservatives did not affect attractancy.

Cydnids were also collected from flight and emergence traps, although they were relatively much less abundant in these latter two types of traps.

Family: Dipsocoridae

Dipsocoridae, or jumping ground bugs, are minute bugs (1.0–1.5 mm in length) with long, thin antennae, which live in moist soil litter. They were the second most common family of Heteroptera in our samples, after their close relatives, the Schizopteridae. Because dipsocorids live predominantly on the forest floor, relatively few were seen in light and flight trap samples, but accounted for 11% of hemipterans in emergence traps and almost half of all hemipterans in the baited pitfall

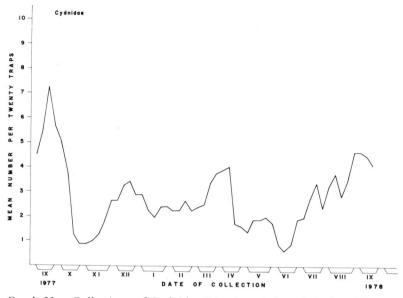

Graph 23. Collections of Cydnidae (Hemiptera) from baited pitfall traps.

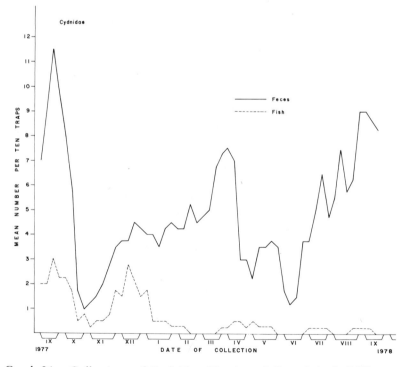

Graph 24. Collections of Cydnidae (Hemiptera) from baited pitfall traps, segregated by bait.

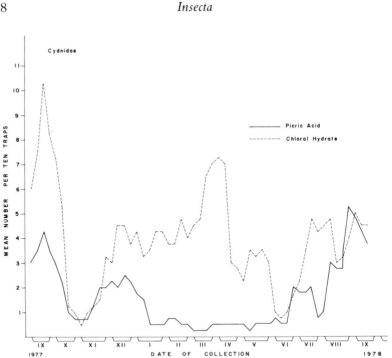

Graph 25.   Collections of Cydnidae (Hemiptera) from baited pitfall traps,
           segregated by preservatives.

traps. Their small size, however, precluded their contributing
significantly to arthropod biomass of these pitfall trap samples.

Although dipsocorids were present throughout the year, pitfall trap records indicate a strikingly sharp November emergence of these bugs in 1977. Interestingly, this mass emergence
was recorded almost completely in traps baited with feces; traps
with fish continued through the month of November with
"normally" low numbers (graph 26). Statistically, feces was
very significantly more attractive to Dipsocoridae (P < .001)
while preservatives showed no significant difference in
attractancy.

Family: Enicocephalidae
Enicocephalidae, or unique-headed bugs, are elongate, flattened, predaceous bugs with a distinctively lobed pronotum
and entirely membranous forewings. They were only rarely
encountered in Reserva Ducke; three were collected from 1 m

light traps and four in emergence traps. This seems to indicate a presence near or at ground level. The three enicocephalids in light traps were collected on 1 Nov. 1977, 4 Apr. 1978, and 27 Sept. 1978. Specimens were collected from emergence traps on 24 Jan., 21 Feb., 6 June, and 13 Sept. 1978.

Family: Lygaeidae

Lygaeidae, or seed bugs, are generally small bugs which feed on mature seeds, although a few are predaceous or feed on plant sap. The family is a large one, but more common in grasslands than in forests. At Reserva Ducke, 139 lygaeids were collected utilizing all trapping techniques, although most were encountered in the flight trap. Flight trap data indicate largest catches of this family in early July (graph 27).

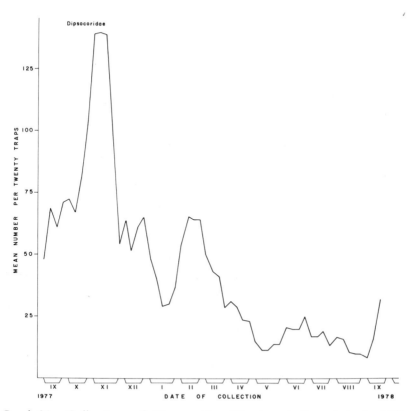

Graph 26. Collections of Dipsocoridae (Hemiptera) from baited pitfall traps.

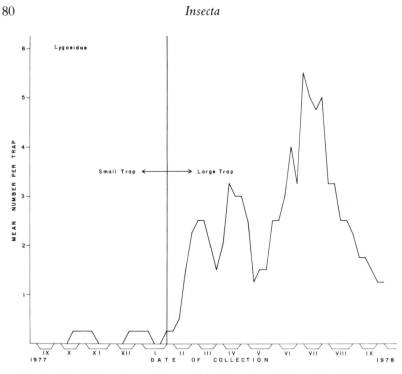

Graph 27.   Collections of Lygaeidae (Hemiptera) from the flight trap.

Family: Mesoveliidae

Mesoveliidae, or water treaders live close to water where they actively run over the moist surfaces of algae, other aquatic plants and objects. This family is easily identified by the membrane of the forewing which continues along the anal margin to the wing base. Only one mesoveliid was encountered during the study—trapped in a 15 m light trap on 1 Aug. 1978. As this was about the driest time of the year, perhaps this single individual was trapped far from water as it migrated to a moister site.

Family: Miridae

Miridae, or plant bugs, is the largest family of Heteroptera. Most species feed on plant juices and can cause considerable damage. A few species are predaceous on other insects. Mirids are small, frequently brightly colored, and have a distinctive cuneus on the forewing corium.

Plant bugs were commonly collected in the traps, and in the

flight trap accounted for almost 8% of all Hemiptera (graph 28). They were more than 10 times as abundant in light traps in the tree canopy as at ground level. The 15 m light trap data (graph 29) reveal a strongly seasonal emergence in late November in the canopy. This peak was not noted in the smaller sample at ground level.

Family: Nabidae

Nabidae, or damsel bugs, are small, brown, predatory bugs which closely resemble some Reduviidae. Damsel bugs are most commonly encountered in grasslands, but a total of 12 individuals were collected—11 of them in the flight trap. All 11 individuals in the flight trap were collected between mid-June and the end of September.

Family: Pentatomidae

Pentatomidae, or stinkbugs, are shield-shaped, medium-sized insects which release a strong chemical odor when disturbed. The family is a large one with several pest species. Stinkbugs

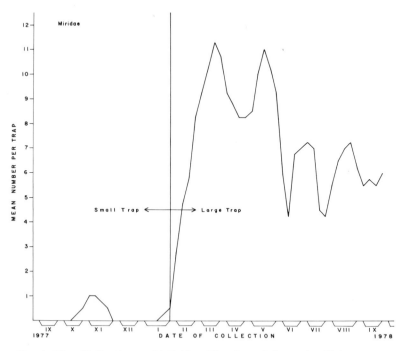

Graph 28.   Collections of Miridae (Hemiptera) from the flight trap.

feed on plant fluids, or other insects, and some species will feed
on either, facultatively. Only two pentatomids were collected
during the study, both in the flight trap on 28 Feb. and 20 June.

Family: Reduviidae

Reduviidae, or assassin bugs, is a large family of medium sized
to large, predaceous insects (fig. 32). They can generally be
recognized by the short, conical beak. Most reduviids are predaceous on other insects, but some species of the subfamily
Triatominae will bite man and are vectors of *Trypanosoma cruzi*,
the causative agent of Chagas' Disease, or American Sleeping
Sickness.

   Reduviidae was encountered in all types of traps, but never
in very large numbers that are seen in some plant feeding families. Altogether, they accounted for only a little over 1% of
hemipterous insects from our samples, and in terms of biomass
were too infrequently present to be significant.

   One of the more interesting subfamilies is Emesinae (Ploia-
riinae), often called thread-legged bugs, which are occasionally
accorded family status. Members of this subfamily are extremely long and thin, making them appear almost invisible at
times. Emesinae are predominantly tropical in distribution, although found in all biogeographical regions, and Wygodzinsky
(1966) lists 86 genera in six tribes worldwide.

   In the present study, Emesinae were frequently encountered.
For example, over half of the Reduviidae collected from light

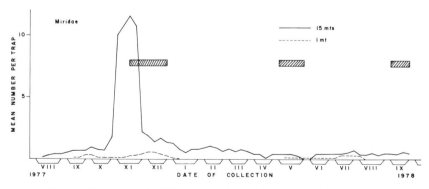

Graph 29.   Collections of Miridae (Hemiptera) from 1 and 15 m light traps.

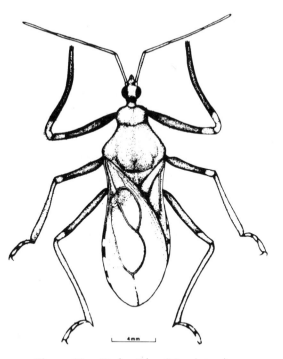

Figure 32.   Reduviidae (Hemiptera).

traps were Emesinae, about evenly dispersed between ground level and canopy. Their presence in the traps was noted throughout the year at low populational levels.

Family: Schizopteridae

Schizopteridae, or jumping ground bugs, are closely related to Dipsocoridae, and like them inhabit the forest litter. They are small (1.0 to 1.5 mm in length) and seldom encountered in temperate climates (fig. 33). However, on the forest floor at Reserva Ducke they are quite abundant, accounting for over 18% of all Hemiptera in the various traps. To pinpoint their numbers a little more closely, they represent 71% of all heteropterans in the 15 m light traps and 60% of heteropterans in all light traps. Schizopteridae and Dipsocoridae together make up 71% of all Hemiptera in the baited pitfall traps.

One surprising morphological note on Schizopteridae is the occurrence of large numbers of heavily sclerotized, wingless females in the population. They look like very small beetles (fig. 33), until the segmented beak is noted.

Data from light trap catches indicates that although this family is known to be ground dwelling, much higher catches were achieved in the canopy, indicating a presence in the treetops. The same data (graph 30) indicates a peak emergence in Sept.–Oct. 1977, with secondary emergences in December and April. The emergence peak did not occur in Sept. 1978 in the same light traps. Baited pitfall data (graphs 31, 32) indicate a strong October emergence for both sclerotized females and non-sclerotized adults.

Family: Scutellaridae

Scutellaridae, or shield-backed bugs, are closely related to Pentatomidae and have similar habits. They can be quickly recognized by the expanded scutellum that extends back and almost covers the wings. Only one scutellarid was encountered during the study, in a flight trap on 20 June.

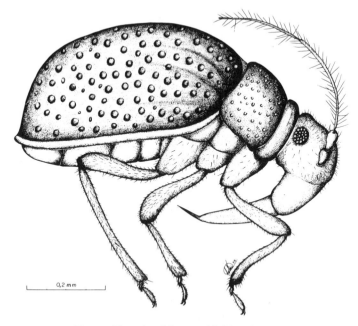

0,2 mm

Figure 33.   A schizopterid (Hemiptera).

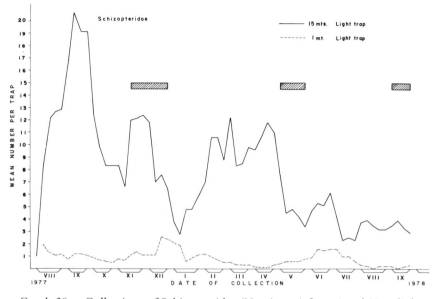

Graph 30.   Collections of Schizopteridae (Hemiptera) from 1 and 15 m light
traps.

Family: Tingidae

Tingidae, or lace bugs, are small, plant-fluid–feeding heteropterans. At times their populations can reach high enough
levels to cause a yellow spotting effect on leaves, and if in higher
populational densities will retard plant growth.

Only 13 lace bugs were encountered at Reserva Ducke, 6 of
them in the emergence traps. Population levels were too low
to identify population trends or biomass contribution.

ORDER: NEUROPTERA

The order Neuroptera includes a highly diverse grouping of
families, all of which are predators. Neuropterans are among
the most primitive of holometabolous orders, with a fossil history which dates back to the early Permian, almost 300 million
years ago. Penny (1977) listed about 1100 species of Neuroptera
in 17 families from South and Central America. One family,
Brucheiseridae, is endemic to Argentina and Chile, while some
others, such as Nemopteridae, Osmylidae and Polystoechotidae

have very relict distributions. There are 10 families of Neuroptera known from the Amazon Basin, two of them mentioned
here for the first time. With the exception of the two aquatic
families, Corydalidae and Sialidae (both of which have been
collected at Reserva Ducke), all Neuroptera families known
from the Amazon Basin were encountered during the study.
Table 17 (see appendix) gives total numbers of collected specimens for the respective families.

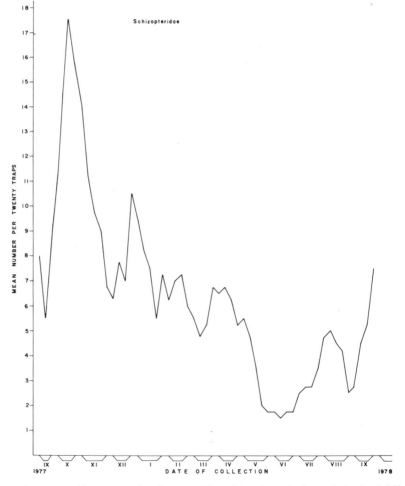

Graph 31. Collections of Schizopteridae (Hemiptera) from baited pitfall
traps.

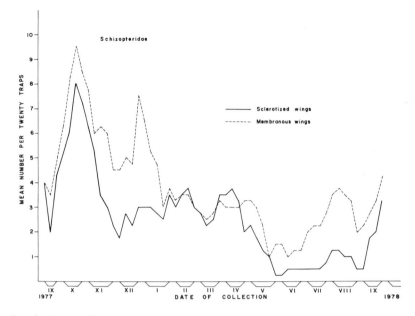

Graph 32.   Collections of Schizopteridae (Hemiptera) from baited pitfall
traps, segregated by wing seclerotization.

Family: Ascalaphidae

Ascalaphidae, or owl-flies, are large insects with a strong re-
semblance to dragonflies, and like them feed on flying insects.
However, unlike dragonflies, owl-flies have long, knobbed
antennae (fig. 34). It has been noted that at Reserva Ducke
adults appear to be most active at dusk, and occasionally cluster
together on branches. Larvae are quite flat and rounded in out-
line, often with cryptic coloration. Generally, during the day
Amazonian ascalaphid larvae remain motionless on leaves with
long mandibles open. At night, they actively run over the leaves
looking for prey.

Ascalaphidae is a fairly large family, with 15 genera and 78
species recorded from continental South America. Penny
(1981b) records 21 species from Amazonia. Only two ascala-
phids were encountered during the study, both larvae which
fell into the baited pitfall traps on 7 and 28 March.

Family: Chrysopidae

Chrysopidae, or green lacewings, are medium to large-sized insects with long antennae, green wings with many crossveins, and shiny golden eyes (fig. 35). When disturbed, many species will give off an unpleasant chemical odor. Larvae are elongate, spiny with prominent mandibles. The immatures feed on aphids and other soft-bodied homopterans which they drain of body fluids with hollow mandibles; then frequently place the body shell of their prey on their backs for camouflage. Lacewing eggs are generally placed singly on the end of a long, stiff thread.

Chrysopidae is one of the largest families of Neuroptera, with 20 genera and 274 species and subspecies described from continental South America, although the family is badly in need of revision. Chrysopidae was the predominant family of Neuroptera encountered during the study. They accounted for almost 60% of all Neuroptera and 67% of Neuroptera from the flight trap. No fluctuations in seasonal distribution could be noted from the present data.

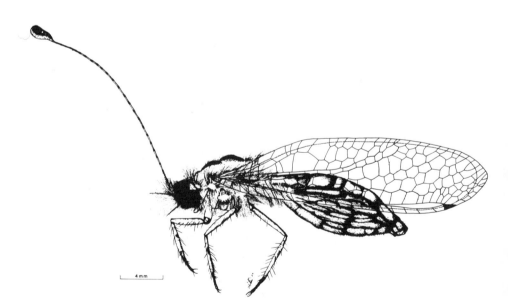

Figure 34.   *Ululodes cajennensis* (Fabr.), Ascalaphidae (Neuroptera).

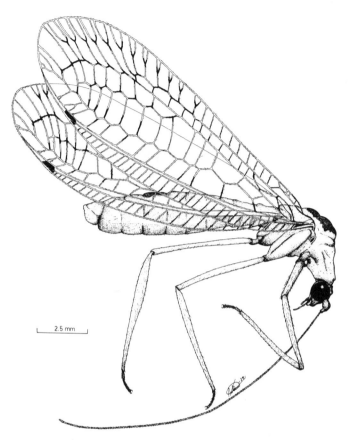

Figure 35. *Leucochrysa varia* (Schneider), Chrysopidae (Neuroptera).

Family: Coniopterygidae

Coniopterygidae, or dusky-wings, are tiny neuropterous insects, which are covered by a gray or white powder (fig. 36). Larvae are elongate, with long, straight mandibles, which they use to capture soft-bodied homopterans.

These insects are seldom encountered due to their small size, but can be locally common. Meinander (1972) in his world revision of the Coniopterygidae recorded five genera and 13 species from South America. In 1973 and 1974 he added five more South American species.

Meinander (1980) has recently taken coniopterygids from this study and a few others from the Manaus area and described 10

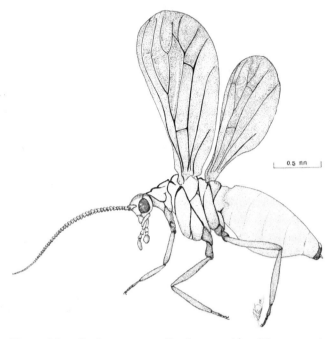

Figure 36.   *Coniopteryx* sp., Coniopterygidae (Neuroptera).

species from Amazonia, nine of them new species. These are
the first records of this family from the Amazon Basin. During
the study nine individuals were collected from 15 m light traps
(4), the flight trap (4), and an emergence trap (1). The latter
capture was probably fortuitous. From this and other data, it
is felt that populations are present in low numbers throughout
the year, and are especially prevalent in the forest canopy, although their presence in the flight trap indicates that they do
move around at ground level.

Family: Dilaridae

Dilaridae, or pleasing lacewings, are small insects with hairy,
pigmented wings. Males have doubly pectinate antennae (fig.
37). Adams (1970) in his revision of New World Dilaridae
placed all American species in the genus *Nallachius* of the
subfamily Nallachiinae. In the geographical section of his revision he states, "there are no known species from the Amazon
Basin. This may merely reflect collecting intensity." It *does*

0.5 mm

Figure 37.   *Nallachius* sp., Dilaridae (Neuroptera).

reflect collecting intensity, and we might add, collecting technique. We encountered 19 dilarids, all in light traps at 15 m height. They appear to be predominantly associated with forest canopy. They also appear to be most prevalent during the driest part of the year, from June through September.

Family: Hemerobiidae

Hemerobiidae, or brown lacewings, are medium-sized insects with brown, heavily crossveined wings (fig. 38). Larvae have habits very similar to Chrysopidae, running actively over plant surfaces in search of soft-bodied insect prey.

Hemerobiidae is a fairly large family, with 12 genera and 59 species recorded from continental South America. They are much more common in temperate zones, and are here recorded for the first time in this century from the Amazon Basin. Altogether, eight individuals were collected, all in light traps, about evenly balanced between canopy and ground level. All but one of these hemerobiids were collected during the months of August and September, indicating an emergence during the height of the dry season.

Family: Mantispidae

Mantispidae, or mantid-flies, are medium-sized, predaceous insects with elongate prothorax and swollen, raptorial forelegs used to capture and hold prey (fig. 39). Larvae are known to be parasitic on spider egg sacs, and have been captured attached

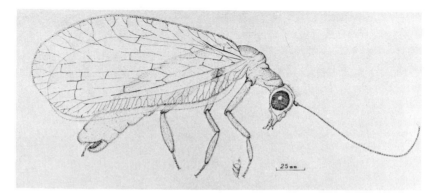

Figure 38.   *Notiobiella* sp., Hemerobiidae (Neuroptera).

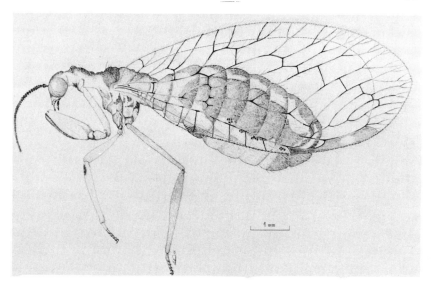

Figure 39. *Trichoscelia* sp., Mantispidae (Neuroptera).

to the bodies of wolf spiders, Lycosidae. Linsley and MacSwain (1955) and Parker and Stange (1965) report mantispid larvae parasitizing bee and wasp nest cells, while Werner (1962) reports mantispid larvae associated with scarab beetle pupae. It appears that mantid-flies, as a family have the ability to parasitize a wide variety of arthropods.

Mantispidae is a fairly large family, with 12 genera and 84 species known from South America. In all, 59 mantispids were encountered during the study, all from the subfamily Platymantispinae. A few individuals were found in light and emergence traps, but the overwhelming majority came from the flight trap. Flight trap records (graph 33) indicate a May emergence peak of this family, although they can be found at all times of the year.

Family: Myrmeleontidae

Myrmeleontidae, or ant lions, are large, long-winged neuropterans (fig. 40). Adults are slow-flying and often attracted to light. Some larvae dig funnels in dry, loose sand or soil where they wait buried in the bottom sand for ants and other ground-dwelling arthropods to fall in; whereupon they are immediately

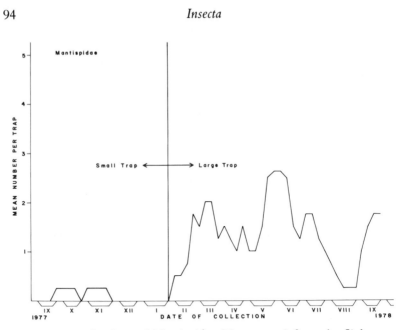

Graph 33.   Collections of Mantispidae (Neuroptera) from the flight trap.

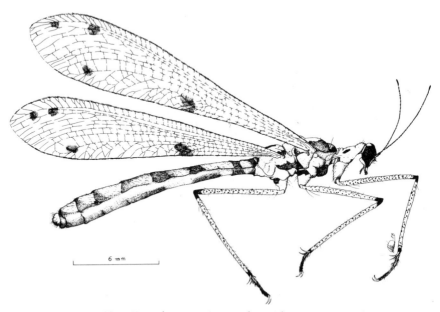

Figure 40.   *Eremoleon* sp., Myrmeleontidae (Neuroptera).

seized and body fluids sucked out through hollow mandibles. They are more common in dry areas where loose, dry, sandy soil is prevalent. However, other larvae are active predators seeking out prey, and one species is known to be a mutillid wasp mimic (Brach 1978).

Myrmeleontidae is a quite large family, with 34 genera and 122 species known from continental South America. During the study, only three ant lions were captured; one in a 15 m light trap on 27 Sept. and two in the flight trap on 28 Feb. and 25 July.

Family: Sisyridae

Sisyridae, or spongilla flies, are small aquatic insects as larvae, which are attracted to lights as adults (fig. 41). Larvae are parasitic on freshwater sponges of the genus *Spongilla*.

Sisyridae is a very small family, confined mainly to tropical waters. Parfin and Gurney (1956) listed only 42 species and 4 genera for the whole world. Two genera and 11 species have been recorded from South America. Penny (1981a) records two genera and 8 species from Amazonia. This family was not taken

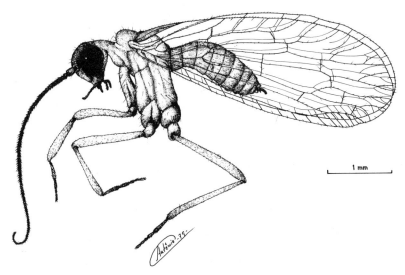

Figure 41. *Sisyra apicalis* Banks, Sisyridae (Neuroptera).

during the study until the last week (Oct. 3), when one individual was encountered in a 15 m light trap. Other collections in the Manaus area have been made long distances from water and freshwater sponges, indicating that adult spongilla flies can migrate long distances, or that we need more studies of larval habits.

ORDER: COLEOPTERA

Coleoptera, or beetles, are the largest order of insects, with about 40% of all described forms. They vary in size from the largest insect in the world, *Titanus giganteus*, to a size so small they are hard to see with the unaided eye. They live in almost every conceivable habitat, from water to soil, to tree trunks, to other insects, to lead cables. Beetles are generally recognizable by the heavily sclerotized forewings, called elytra, but in some families, such as Lycidae, the sclerotization in reduced, and in other families, such as Staphylinidae and Pselaphidae, the sclerotized elytra may be reduced in size to small pads. Additionally, a few other groups have developed highly sclerotized wings, such as female Schizopteridae. However, *almost* always a highly sclerotized forewing indicates a beetle.

There is some disagreement among specialists as to the classification of Coleoptera. We have followed that of Arnett (1968) because of the included keys which allow association of insect with standardized name. His keys to families of beetles of the world includes 124 families.

During the study 74 families of beetles were collected, some of them only a few times, others so frequently that, like with the Staphylinidae, total numbers surpassed 100,000 individuals. In terms of total numbers, Coleoptera accounted for from 1.6% of insects in the 1 m light traps to 25% of all arthropods in baited pitfall traps. In terms of arthropod biomass, beetles were a very important component of the tropical forest ecosystem. Over a third of all arthropods, by weight, emerging from the soil were beetles. About one-eighth of all arthropods, by weight, trapped in the flight trap were beetles. However, most impressive were the baited pitfall traps with protein sources— from 67 to 96% of all arthropods, by weight, were beetles.

Family: Alleculidae

Alleculidae, or comb-clawed beetles, are medium-sized, somewhat elongate, often metallic-colored beetles with characteristic dentate claws (fig. 42). Adults are frequently seen clinging to foliage of shrubs, where they probably feed on pollen.

There are about 1200 known species of Alleculidae worldwide.

Fifty-seven alleculids were collected during the study, primarily in the flight and emergence traps. Adults were collected in the flight trap most frequently in May–June while emergence traps indicated a scattered emergence from November to July.

Family: Anobiidae

Anobiidae, or deathwatch beetles, are small (2–6 mm.), oval insects with deeply deflexed head (fig. 43). These insects are often pests of wood-paneling, book bindings, cigars and cigarettes, and stored food products.

There are about 1200 anobiid species described, worldwide.

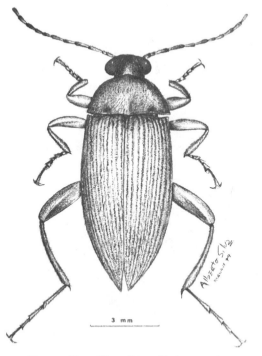

3 mm

Figure 42. Alleculidae (Coleoptera).

Anobiids were collected using all trapping methods, except baited pitfall traps. There were more than five times as many deathwatch beetles collected with lights in the forest canopy as at ground level.

Family: Anthicidae

Anthicidae, or ant-like flower beetles, are small beetles with deflexed head, entire eyes, and prominent pronotum (fig. 44). They are frequently encountered visiting flowers.

Anthicidae is a medium-sized family with almost 2000 described species. In Reserva Ducke, a total of 26 anthicids were collected, almost all in light traps. They were more than three times as common in the forest canopy as at ground level.

Family: Anthribidae

Anthribidae, or fungus weevils, are closely related to weevils, but can be separated by the broad snout and non-geniculated antennae (fig. 45). Frequently, the antennae are extremely long.

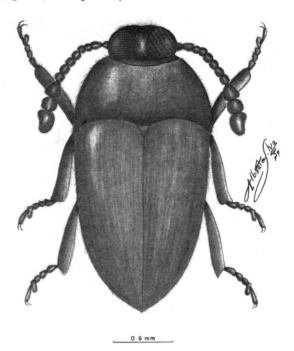

0.6 mm

Figure 43.   Anobiidae (Coleoptera).

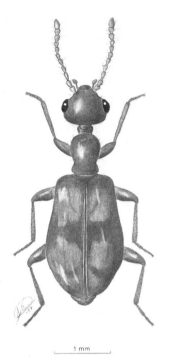

1 mm

Figure 44.   Anthicidae (Coleoptera).

In size, arthribids vary from 1 to 30 mm. They usually have a mottled gray or brown coloration, and are most often seen on tree trunks where they blend very well with the background. They fly readily when disturbed, with long antennae extended in a manner resembling Cerambycidae.

Anthribidae is a fairly large family with about 2500 species described.

At Reserva Ducke, 37 anthribids were encountered, 35 of them in the flight trap. They appeared to be most abundant in February, although they could be collected at any time of the year.

Family: Biphyllidae

Biphyllidae, or false skin beetles, are small (2–3 mm), hairy beetles (fig. 46) which look very much like Mycetophagidae and Cryptophagidae, but can be separated from these other two families by the prosternum not being prolonged behind in Biphyllidae. This family is found in fungus and under bark, where they are probably fungus feeders.

Biphyllidae is a small family with only 200 described forms.

Only six biphyllids were taken at Reserva Ducke, three of them in the 1 m light trap.

Family: Bostrichidae

Bostrichidae, or bostrichid powder-post beetles, are elongate, dark brown beetles of medium size, usually 2 to 20 mm. They normally have a deflexed head and tuberculate pronotum (fig. 47). They appear similar to Scolytidae, but have straight antennae and five segmented tarsi. Larvae are usually wood-boring, but can also be found in thatch roofs in the Amazon.

Bostrichidae is a small family with only about 450 described species.

These beetles were only encountered four times during the study: in a 1 m light trap on 22 Nov.; two in 15 m light traps

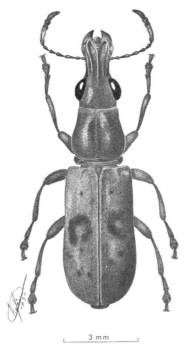

3 mm

Figure 45.   Anthribidae (Coleoptera).

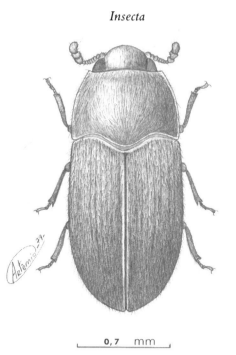

Figure 46. Biphyllidae (Coleoptera).

on 29 Nov. and 14 Feb.; and one in an emergence trap on 13 Dec.

Family: Brentidae

Brentidae, or straight-snouted weevils, are medium to large-sized (10 to 30 mm) black or dark brown beetles with a long, straight snout (fig. 48). The form of the snout is characteristic for this family and the length can vary greatly within a species. They are almost always encountered in rotten logs, where adults sometimes live in groups.

This family is fairly large, with about 1300 species described.

Nineteen brentids were collected at Reserva Ducke: 12 in the 15 m light traps and seven in the flight trap. They could be collected in low numbers throughout the year.

Family: Bruchidae

Bruchidae, or bean weevils, are small to medium-sized beetles with oval bodies, small heads, and long antennae (fig. 49). They feed on plant seeds where they have drawn a good deal of recent attention for their dominant role in tropical "seed predation" (Janzen 1971).

Bean weevils are a fairly large family with about 1300 known species worldwide.

Only six bruchids were collected during the study, probably due to the trapping techniques utilized. Two individuals were collected in 15 m light traps on 21 Feb. and 16 May. Three bruchids were collected in the flight trap on 20 June, 18 July, and 29 August. One additional specimen was collected from an emergence trap on 11 Oct.

Family: Buprestidae
Buprestidae, or metallic wood-boring beetles, are small to large (3 to 100 mm) in size, elongate-oval in shape, bearing a small

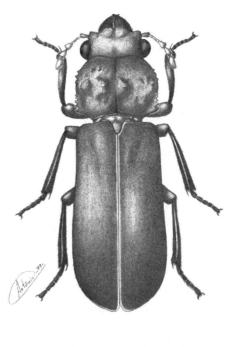

3 mm

Figure 47.   Bostrichidae (Coleoptera).

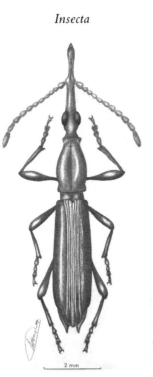

2 mm

Figure 48.   Brentidae (Coleoptera).

depressed head (fig. 50). All are brightly metallic in coloration, and hence a popular taxonomic group.

Larvae burrow through wood, mine leaves, or form galls. Adults feed on foliage or fungus. A few species are of economic importance because of the damage they cause to wood.

The family is a large one with more than 12,000 species known worldwide. However, in Reserva Ducke only 28 individuals were collected, 25 of them in the flight trap. The flight trap used early in the study failed to trap any buprestids, while the later trap caught them at a consistently low but continuous rate from February through September. The buprestid contribution to the biomass appeared to be very low.

Family: Byrrhidae

Byrrhidae, or pill beetles, are small (5 to 10 mm), convex beetles with deflexed head (fig. 51). Adults and larvae are herbivorous in a wide variety of situations, and when disturbed can retract appendages and remain motionless.

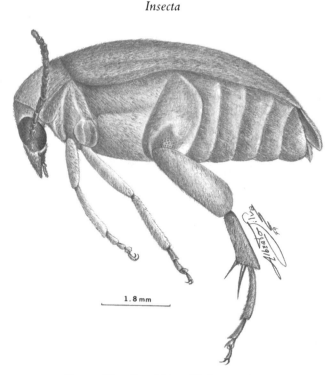

Figure 49. Bruchidae (Coleoptera).

Byrrhidae is a small family with only about 280 described species, and only seven individuals were collected at Reserva Ducke. All were collected in light traps, about evenly balanced between 1 and 15 m. All were collected on 30 Aug. and 6 Sept. 1977.

Family: Cantharidae

Cantharidae, or soldier beetles, are small to medium-sized (1 to 15 mm), elongate beetles with deflexed head not hidden by pronotum (fig. 52). Larvae are predaceous on other insects, while adults can often be seen resting on the forest vegetation.

The family is medium-sized, with more than 3500 species described worldwide.

Cantharids were commonly encountered in all traps at Reserva Ducke, except the pitfall traps. They were especially common in the flight trap where 158 individuals were collected. There appeared to be two collection peaks in the flight trap;

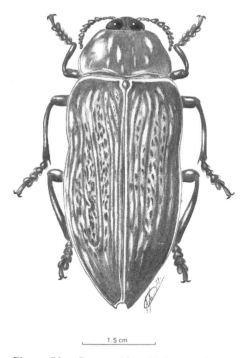

1.5 cm

Figure 50.   Buprestidae (Coleoptera).

0.1 mm

Figure 51.   Byrrhidae (Coleoptera).

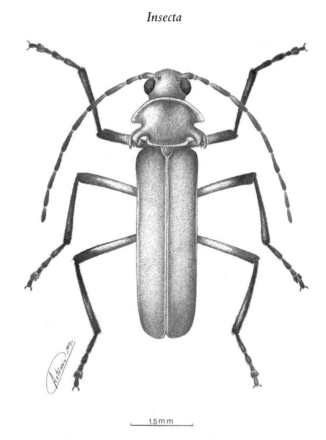

1.5 mm

Figure 52.   Cantharidae (Coleoptera).

first in April, then again in September (graph 34). Emergence trap data shows emergences from the soil in December, March, and late May (graph 35). However, soldier beetles' contribution to overall beetle biomass was very small.

Family: Carabidae

Carabidae, or ground beetles, are small to large-sized (3 to 85 mm), elongate, oval beetles with prognathous head and relatively large mandibles (fig. 53). They can be readily identified as one of the few families of active, terrestrial beetles with posterior coxae dividing the first abdominal sternum. Color normally varies from black to fuscous to metallic green, and some species can be brightly colored. Both adults and larvae

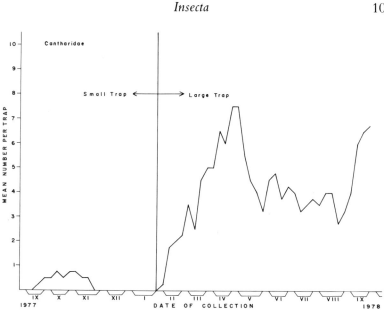

Graph 34. Collections of Cantharidae (Coleoptera) from the flight trap.

are generally predaceous on other insects, although larvae of some temperate species of *Clivina* and *Agonoderus* can destroy seed-corn at planting time, and some tropical American species of *Calophaena* tunnel through stems of *Heliconia* as larvae (Terry Erwin, personal communication).

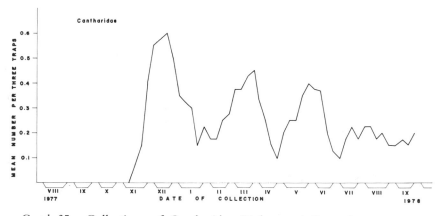

Graph 35. Collections of Cantharidae (Coleoptera) from the emergence traps.

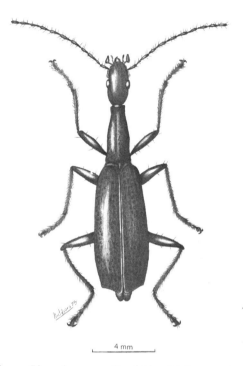

Figure 53. *Agra* sp., Carabidae (Coleoptera).

Ground beetles are one of the largest families of beetles, with about 25,000 species worldwide. Although primarily known as forest floor dwellers, at Reserva Ducke almost eight times as many carabids were collected in light traps in the forest canopy as at ground level. However, this does not mean that they are absent from the forest floor. They accounted for more than 6% of all beetles collected in the flight trap (although they may not have flown into the trap, but rather run up the sides). Many ground beetles were also collected in emergence (graph 38) and pitfall traps. Both light trap and flight trap data (graphs 36, 37) indicate a March population peak. In terms of arthropod biomass however, Carabidae made up a very small proportion of the whole biomass.

Family: Cerambycidae

Cerambycidae, or long-horned wood borers, are generally small to very large, elongate beetles characterized by the long antennae (fig. 54). Many are brown or black, but some are red or metallic colored. The largest beetle in the world, *Titanus giganteus*, is a member of this family, known from the Manaus region of the central Amazon Basin. Larvae bore through wood and roots, while adults may feed on a wide variety of foods.

Cerambycidae is a large family, with more than 20,000 species known worldwide. They were frequently taken at Reserva Ducke where, because of their size, were readily noted. Altogether 206 individuals of Cerambycidae were encountered, eight of them in light traps, and seven of them in 15 m light traps (graph 39). All eight individuals in the light traps were collected between September and December.

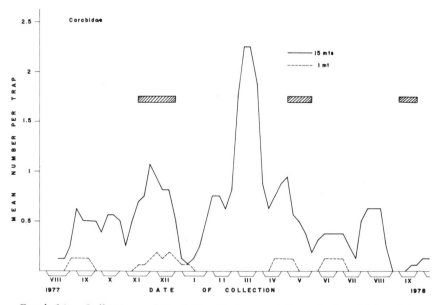

Graph 36.   Collections of Carabidae (Coleoptera) from the 1 and 15 m light traps.

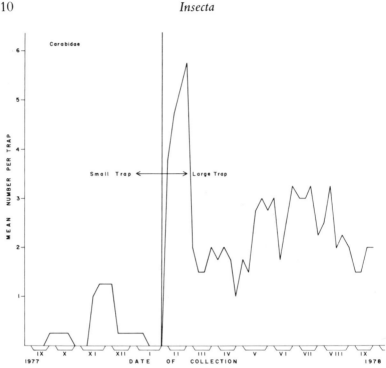

Graph 37.   Collections of Carabidae (Coleoptera) from the flight trap.

Family: Chelonariidae

Chelonariidae, or chelonariid beetles, are dark, oval beetles whose head and appendages fit so well into the heavily sclerotized body that when retracted, only the eyes and mandibles are visible and antennae and legs are difficult to discern (fig. 55). Larvae are aquatic and adults are found on leaves.

Chelonariidae is a very small family with less than 50 known species.

During the study, ten adults were encountered, eight of them in light traps, and seven of them in 15 m light traps. All eight individuals in the light traps were collected between September and December.

Family: Chrysomelidae

Chrysomelidae, or leaf beetles, are a very diverse group of beetles, who generally feed on leaves or roots of plants, both

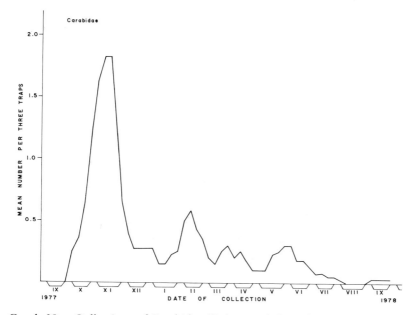

Graph 38. Collections of Carabidae (Coleoptera) from the emergence traps.

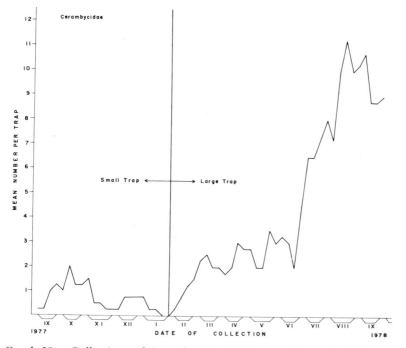

Graph 39. Collections of Cerambycidae (Coleoptera) from the flight trap.

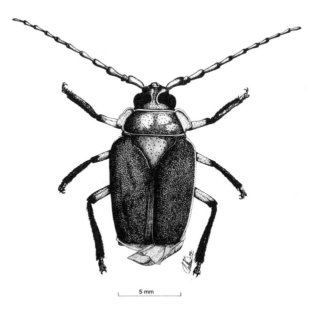

5 mm

Figure 54.   *Pyrodes laetificus* Bates, Cerambycidae (Coleoptera).

as larvae and adults. They have a bilobed third tarsal segment of all legs and fairly short antennae (fig. 56). Because of their leaf-feeding habits, they can defoliate a tree, and many species are considered serious pests of crops.

Chrysomelidae is a very large family, with more than 20,000 described species. In Reserva Ducke, 2852 leaf beetles were collected, accounting for a little over 1% of the total beetles and more than 16% of the beetles in the flight trap. However, because of their generally smaller size, leaf beetles never accounted for more than 1% of the beetle biomass in any of the traps.

Seasonally, chrysomelids were most often caught in 15 m light traps in late January, but collections at 1 m light traps remained low at this time (graph 40). Perhaps this differential result reflects the greater quantity of new foliage in the forest

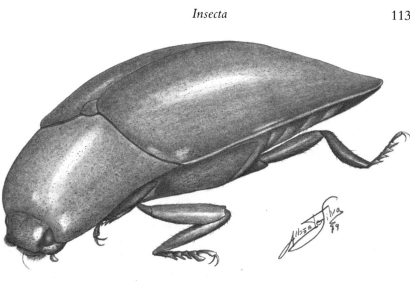

1.4 mm

Figure 55.   Chelonariidae (Coleoptera).

canopy. Emergence traps indicated higher population levels between November and January (graph 41).

Family: Cisidae

Cisidae, or minute tree-fungus beetles, are tiny (2 to 3 mm), cylindrical beetles which live gregariously on shelf-fungi and in rotten wood. They resemble small scolytids, but can be separated by the non-geniculated antennae (fig. 57).

The family is a small one, with only about 250 species known worldwide. A total of five cisids were collected during the

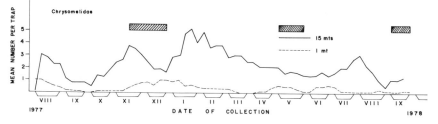

Graph 40.   Collections of Chrysomelidae (Coleoptera) from 1 and 15 m light traps.

Insecta

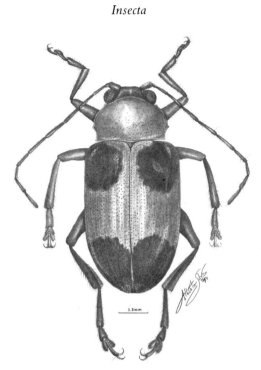

Figure 56.   Chrysomelidae (Coleoptera).

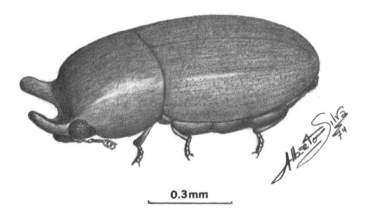

0.3mm

Figure 57.   Cisidae (Coleoptera).

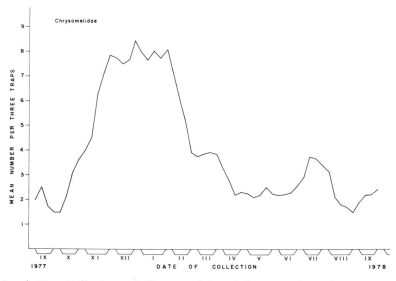

Graph 41.   Collections of Chrysomelidae (Coleoptera) from the emergence
traps.

study, two in 15 m light traps on Nov. 15 and May 9 and three
in emergence traps on Dec. 27, Jan. 17, and Feb. 28. These five
records may indicate a higher population level during the rainy
season from November to May.

Family: Cleridae

Cleridae, or checkered beetles, are cylindrical, brightly colored,
hairy beetles about 3 to 24 mm in length (fig. 58). Most larvae
and adults are predaceous on other insects, but some species
feed on pollen.

The family is fairly large, with about 3500 species known
worldwide. At Reserva Ducke only 25 clerids were collected,
23 of them in the flight trap. Records from the flight trap
indicate that the majority of individuals were taken during the
dry season from June to October.

Family: Coccinellidae

Coccinellidae, or ladybird beetles, are small to medium-sized
(0.8 to 10 mm), rounded beetles that are black, white, red or
orange in coloration, often with spotting on the elytra (fig. 59).

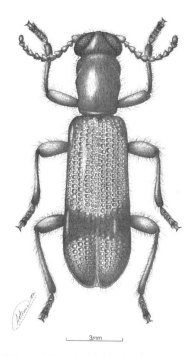

Figure 58.   Cleridae (Coleoptera).

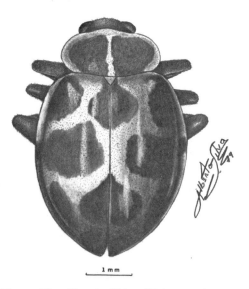

Figure 59.   Coccinellidae (Coleoptera).

They have an appearance very similar to some Chrysomelidae and Erotylidae, but can be generally separated from these families by the metacoxal arcs, broader pronotum and non-flattened apical antennal segments.

Both larvae and adults are usually predaceous on other insects, although some are plant feeders, and one European species is known to develop in horse and cattle manure.

The family is a fairly large one with about 5000 species known worldwide. In Reserva Ducke, 115 ladybird beetles were collected, 106 of them in the flight trap. They seem to be present in the flight trap in consistently low numbers throughout the year. However, biomass was too low to be recorded.

Family: Colydiidae

Colydiidae, or cylindrical bark beetles, are elongate and cylindrical with a two or three-segmented apical antennal club (fig. 60). They normally have a brown or piceus coloration.

Many larvae and adults are predaceous, living under bark or in the galleries of their prey insects. Some are phytophagous,

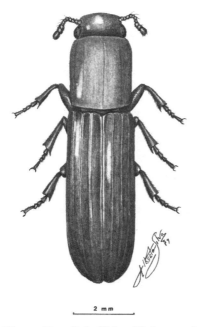

2 mm

Figure 60.   Colydiidae (Coleoptera).

and a few larvae are parasitic on larvae and pupae of Cerambycidae, Buprestidae or Curculionidae.

Less than 1500 species have been described in this family.
Thirty-seven colydiids were encountered in Reserva Ducke,
being caught infrequently in all types of traps. No seasonal
trend in emergence could be discerned.

Family: Cryptophagidae

Cryptophagidae, or silken fungus beetles, are small (1 to 5 mm),
hairy, oval beetles with a three-segmented antennal club (fig.
61). Larvae and adults feed on mold, fungus, decaying vegetation and similar materials. They are sometimes found associated with colonies of social insects, perhaps as scavengers.

The family is a small one, with less than 900 species described
worldwide. Twenty-six individuals were collected in Reserva
Ducke, primarily in the 15 m light traps. There appeared to be
a trend towards higher catches between September and December, but the total number of individuals was too small for definite conclusions to be drawn.

Family: Cucujidae

Cucujidae, or flat bark beetles, are small to medium-sized (2
to 12 mm), flattened beetles with prominent mandibles and

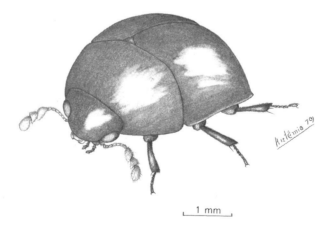

1 mm

Figure 61.   Cryptophagidae (Coleoptera).

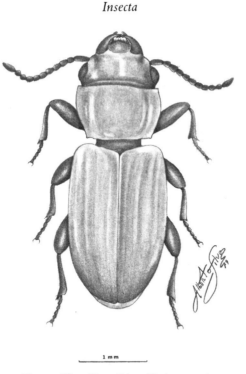

Figure 62.   Cucujidae (Coleoptera).

open mesocoxal cavities (fig. 62). Larvae and adults live under tree bark, on fruit, and in decaying vegetation.

This is a fairly large family with a little more than 5000 species described worldwide. Sixty-four individuals were collected at Reserva Ducke, primarily in the light traps and emergence traps. Almost three times as many cucujids were light trapped at 15 m as at 1 m. The light trap data indicates a sharp increase in catches of this family between 22 Nov. and 20 Dec. Their gregarious nature is emphasized when it is noted that in emergence traps 60% of the individuals were collected in 11% of the traps.

Family: Curculionidae

Curculionidae, or weevils, are a diverse group of beetles ranging in size from 1 to 35 mm. Generally they are rounded, heavily sclerotized beetles with a prominent snout bearing geniculated antennae (fig. 63). Larvae and adults are phytophagous, where they attack almost all plant parts. Many are serious pests of crops and ornamental plants.

This is perhaps the largest family of beetles with more than 60,000 species in 80 subfamilies described worldwide. In Reserva Ducke 894 weevils were collected, especially from the flight trap where they accounted for more than 7% of all beetles encountered. Weevils appeared to be most abundant between Feb. and May in the flight trap (graph 42). However, light trap and emergence trap data indicate higher population levels in August (graphs 43, 44).

Family: Dascillidae

Dascillidae, or soft-bodied plant beetles, are elongate, dark brown beetles of medium size (3 to 14 mm in length). They resemble some Chrysomelidae and Ptilodactylidae, but can be

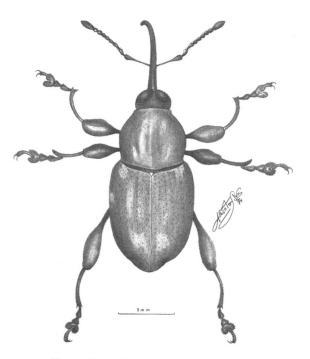

Figure 63.   Curculionidae (Coleoptera).

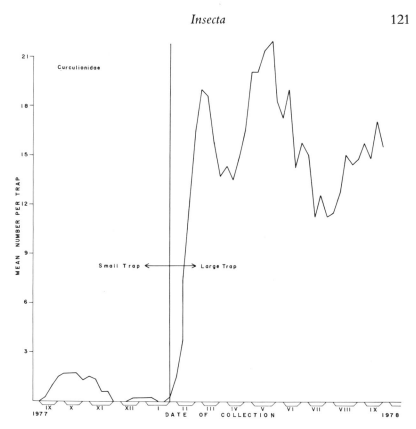

Graph 42.   Collections of Curculionidae (Coleoptera) from the flight trap.

readily separated from these latter families by the lobes on the
first tarsal segments (fig. 64). Larvae live in the soil and adults
are found on foliage near water courses. Adults are probably
predaceous.

Dascillidae is a small family of less than 50 species. However,
in Reserva Ducke they acccounted for more than 1% of all
beetles collected in the flight trap. A total of 136 individuals
were encountered in flight and emergence traps. Emergence of
this family was clear-cut and dramatic. The first dascillids began
emerging from the emergence traps (graph 46) on 18 July after
more than 10 months of negative collections for this family.
Collections continued in these traps until 8 Aug. As this type
of trap is designed for insects to freely enter the collector-pre-
servative area of the trap, some individuals are not collected

Insecta

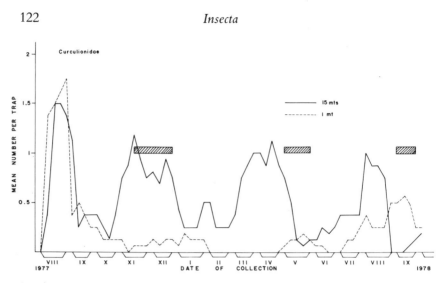

Graph 43.   Collections of Curculionidae (Coleoptera) from 1 and 15 m light
             traps.

right away. That all 13 dascillids were collected within a four
week time span indicates a very narrow emergence range.

The flight trap data (graph 45) indicate similar results. First
catches were made on 18 July, continuing uninterrupted until
13 September, with a peak in mid-August. No other dascillids
were collected outside of this time period.

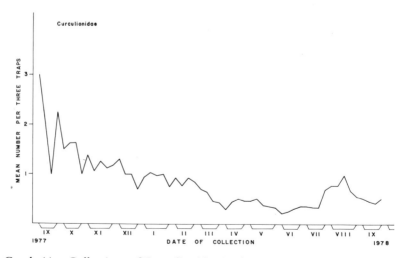

Graph 44.   Collections of Curculionidae (Coleoptera) from emergence traps.

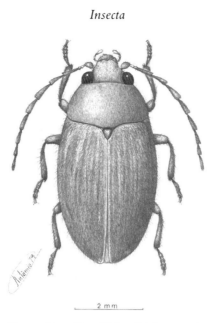

Figure 64.   Dascillidae (Coleoptera).

Family: Dermestidae

Dermestidae, or skin beetles, are small (1 to 12 mm), oval beetles with a compact antennal club. They generally have a dense covering of hairs or scales (fig. 65). Larvae and adults live as scavengers, feeding on dried plant and animal remains. They can be beneficial, cleaning skeletal remains for study of bone structure. For this reason, some museums go to great lengths to eliminate dermestids as pests, while other museums work hard to preserve colonies.

The family is of small size, with about 750 species known worldwide. In Reserva Ducke, skin beetles were most frequently collected from emergence traps, where 25 individuals were encountered. All dermestids were collected between 20 June and 6 Sept., apparently associated with the dry season. The emergence peak appeared to be about 4 July.

Family: Dryopidae

Dryopidae, or long-toed water beetles, are small (1 to 8 mm), elongate, dark, aquatic beetles (fig. 66). Most species are aquatic

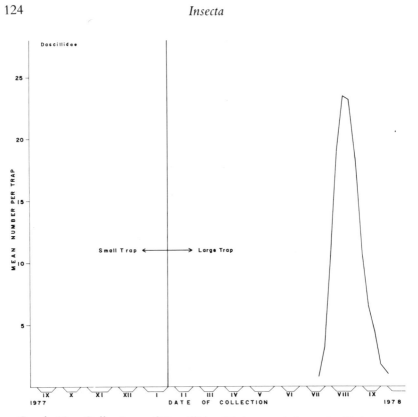

Graph 45.   Collections of Dascillidae (Coleoptera) from the flight trap.

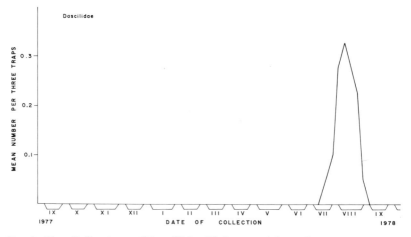

Graph 46.   Collections of Dascillidae (Coleoptera) from the emergence traps.

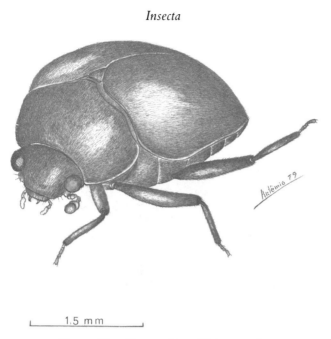

1.5 mm

Figure 65.   Dermestidae (Coleoptera).

as both larvae and adults, crawling along the bottom of streams. However, a few species are terrestrial.

The family is a small one, with only a little over 250 species known worldwide. One dryopid was encountered in Reserva Ducke, collected in an emergence trap on 25 April.

Family: Dytiscidae

Dytiscidae, or predaceous diving beetles, are small to large (1 to 40 mm), heavily sclerotized, rounded beetles (fig. 67). They resemble Hydrophilidae, but can be separated from this latter family by the divided first abdominal sternite and lack of a median sternal keel. Both larvae and adults are aquatic and predaceous, feeding on other aquatic insects.

Dytiscidae is a medium-sized family with more than 4000 species known worldwide. However, only 18 individuals were encountered in Reserva Ducke, principally in the flight trap. Of the 11 specimens collected in the flight trap, all were collected between February and early May.

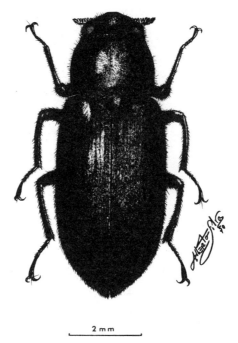

2 mm

Figure 66.   Dryopidae (Coleoptera).

Family: Elateridae

Elateridae, or click beetles, are elongate, depressed beetles with a special morphological structure connecting prosternum and mesosternum, allowing the insect to snap its head and prothorax rapidly forward with a characteristic click (fig. 68). This mechanism allows the beetle to propel itself several centimeters into the air. Larvae and adults are generally herbivorous, the larvae living on rotting vegetation or plant roots where they are known as wireworms. Larvae can often be serious pests of cultivated crops. Adults are usually encountered resting on plant foliage. The common genus *Pyrophorus* in Reserva Ducke has two continuously fluorescent prothoracic spots.

Elateridae is a large family with about 7500 known species worldwide. This was one of the more frequently encountered families in Reserva Ducke, especially in the flight trap where they accounted for more than 13% of all beetles captured. Click beetles accounted for more than 1% of the arthropod biomass in the flight trap, and 42% in 1 m light traps. Flight trap data (graph 47) also indicate a late February emergence peak. Behaviorally, elaterids appear to be one of few families of beetles more common at ground level than in the canopy, as indicated by light trap data. The difference in catches between the two levels was highly significant (P < .001).

Family: Endomychidae

Endomychidae, or handsome fungus beetles, are small (1 to 10 mm) rounded beetles with elongate grooves along the hind margin of the pronotum (fig. 69). Both larvae and adults live in moist situations where they feed on fungus.

The family is a fairly small one with over 1100 described species worldwide. In Reserva Ducke 81 individuals were encountered in light, flight and emergence traps. Light traps at

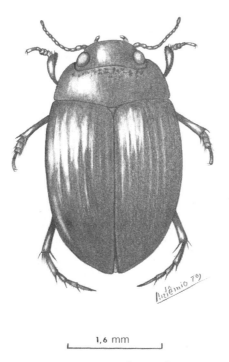

1,6 mm

Figure 67.   Dytiscidae (Coleoptera).

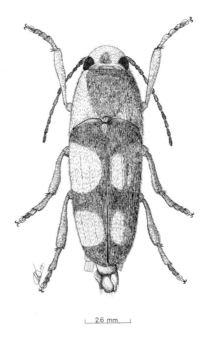

| 2.6 mm. |

Figure 68.   Elateridae (Coleoptera).

15 m indicated highest collections were in mid-November, while emergence traps produced adults from September to April, always at low numbers.

Family: Erotylidae

Erotylidae, or pleasing fungus beetles, are small to medium-sized (3 to 20 mm), heavily sclerotized, elongate to rounded beetles with a three-segmented antennal club (fig. 70). They appear similar to Endomychidae, or sometimes Coccinellidae, but can be separated from the former by lack of elongate grooves on the posterior part of the pronotum, and from the latter family by the more numerous tarsal segments (5-5-5). Larvae and adults occur on fleshy fungus, or within rotten wood.

The family is a fairly small one, with less than 1800 species known worldwide. This was a commonly encountered family in Reserva Ducke, especially in the flight trap. The flight trap

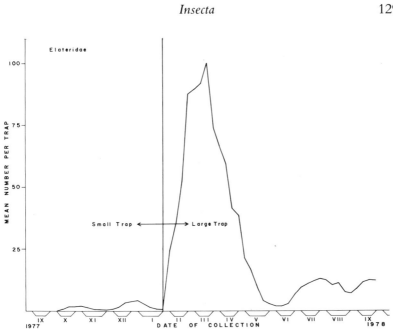

Graph 47.   Collections of Elateridae (Coleoptera) from the flight trap.

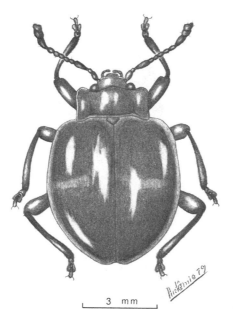

Figure 69.   Endomychidae (Coleoptera).

data indicates a bimodal emergence in March–April and again in September (graph 48).

Family: Eucnemidae

Eucnemidae, or false click beetles, are elongate, dark-colored beetles (fig. 71) of small to medium size (3 to 18 mm). As their common name implies, they resemble Elateridae, but can be separated by the more rounded shape, strongly retracted head, antennal grooves on the propleuron, and poorly developed "click" mechanism of the prosternum.

False click beetles are a small family with only a little over 1000 described species worldwide, but in Reserva Ducke were frequently encountered, especially in light traps and flight trap. Collections in the flight trap were highest in September (graph 49).

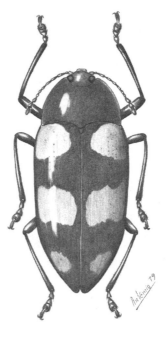

5 mm

Figure 70. *Scaphidomorphus bosci,* Erotylidae (Coleoptera).

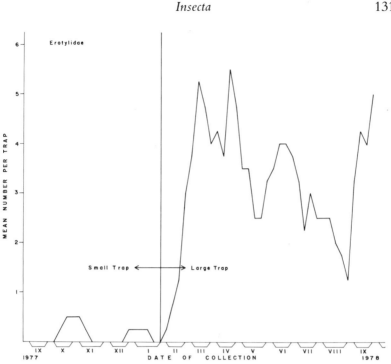

Graph 48.   Collections of Erotylidae (Coleoptera) from the flight trap.

Family: Euglenidae

Euglenidae, or ant-like leaf beetles, are small (1.5 to 3 mm), elongate beetles with large, granulated eyes (fig. 72). They appear somewhat similar to Anthicidae, but can be readily separated by the large eyes and fusion of the first two abdominal segments. Little is known of the biology of this family.

Euglenidae is a small family with less than 800 species described. They were encountered in light, flight and emergence traps in Reserva Ducke, but most frequently in 15 m light traps. Light trap data indicate collections could be made in low numbers throughout the year.

Family: Helodidae

Helodidae, or marsh beetles, are small (2 to 4 mm), oval beetles with expanded hind femora (fig. 73). Larvae of this family are aquatic.

Insecta

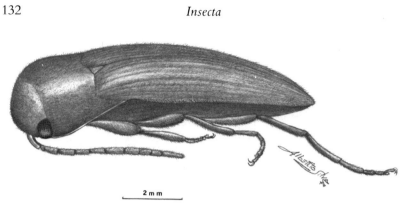

2 mm

Figure 71.   Eucnemidae (Coleoptera).

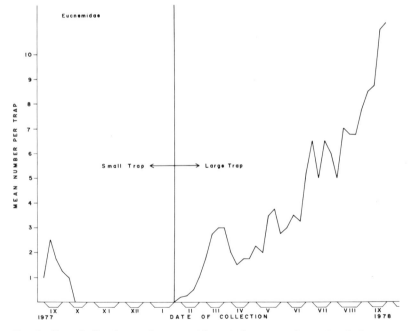

Graph 49.   Collections of Eucnemidae (Coleoptera) from the flight trap.

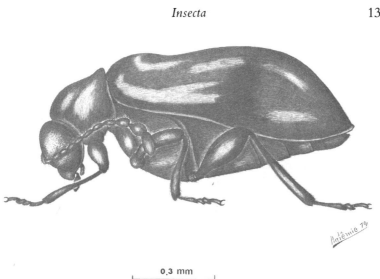

0.3 mm

Figure 72.   Euglenidae (Coleoptera).

Helodidae is a small family of less than 400 known species worldwide. Thirty-five individuals were found at Reserva Ducke, all but one of them in the flight trap. They seemed to be most abundant in the flight trap in June (graph 50).

Family: Histeridae

Histeridae, or hister beetles, are a group of small to medium-sized (0.5 to 10 mm), heavily sclerotized, shiny, black beetles with prominent mandibles, geniculated antennae and short elytra (fig. 74). Adults and larvae are carnivorous or saprophagous, feeding on carrion and excrement.

The family is a fairly large one, with 2500 described species worldwide. At Reserva Ducke, 95 individuals were collected in the emergence traps, but by far the most effective trapping technique was baited pitfall traps. In these pitfall traps, 2339 individuals were collected, or more than 1% of all beetles in the pitfall traps. As shown in graphs 51 and 52, the histerid population appeared to reach a peak in December and January. There was a significant difference ($.005 < P < .01$) in attractancy between fish and feces (graph 53), and a very significant difference in killing-preservative fluids utilized ($P < .001$). It is

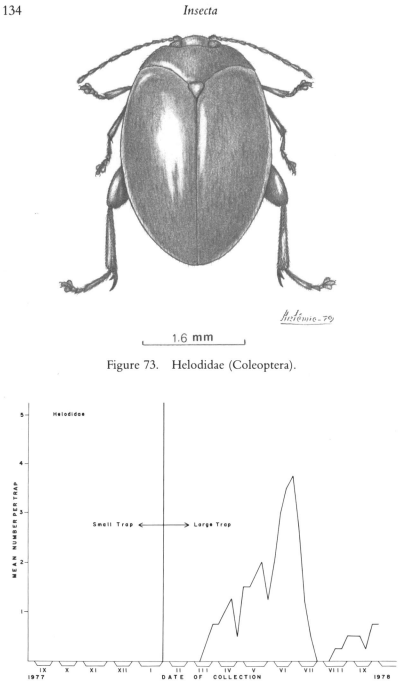

1.6 mm

Figure 73.   Helodidae (Coleoptera).

Graph 50.   Collections of Helodidae (Coleoptera) from the flight trap.

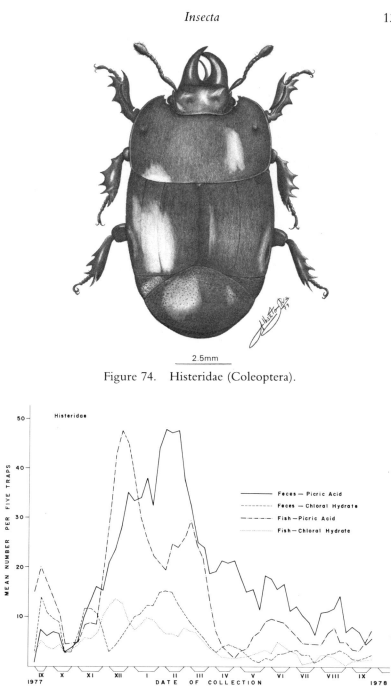

2.5mm

Figure 74.   Histeridae (Coleoptera).

Graph 51.   Collections of Histeridae (Coleoptera) in baited pitfall traps.

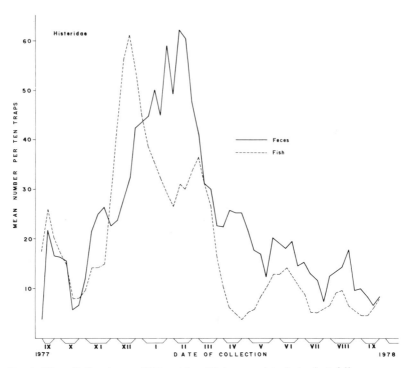

Graph 52.   Collections of Histeridae (Coleoptera) in baited pitfall traps, seg-
              regated by bait.

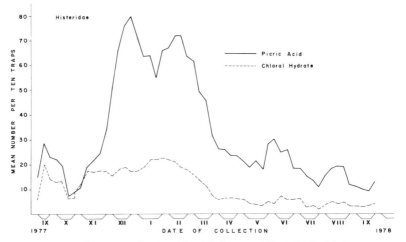

Graph 53.   Collections of Histeridae (Coleoptera) in baited pitfall traps, seg-
              regated by preservatives.

not known whether the picric acid was attracting histerids, or chloral hydrate repelling them. In terms of biomass, in October the dry weight of Histeridae was too small to be significant.

Family: Hydrophilidae

Hydrophilidae, or water scavenger beetles, are dark colored, heavily sclerotized, rounded beetles which resemble Nitidulidae, but have maxillary palpi as long as, or longer than the antennae (fig. 75). Larvae and adults are predaceous, and can be either aquatic or terrestrial. The large number of specimens collected at Reserva Ducke are all terrestrial.

Hydrophilidae is a medium-sized family with around 2000 species known worldwide. Although a few individuas were taken in emergence traps at Reserva Ducke, almost all were taken from baited pitfall traps—a total of 5863 individuals. This family accounted for more than 2% of all beetles collected in pitfall traps. Graphs 54 and 55 indicate the seasonal population trends within the Hydrophilidae, with a February peak emerg-

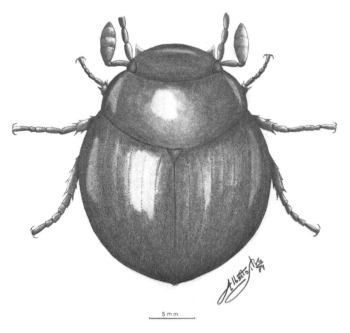

5 m m

Figure 75.   Hydrophilidae (Coleoptera).

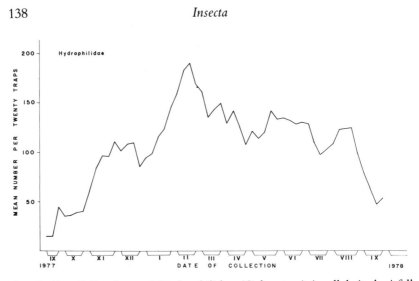

Graph 54.　Collections of Hydrophilidae (Coleoptera) in all baited pitfall traps.

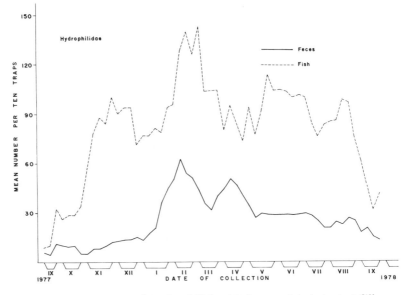

Graph 55.　Collections of Hydrophilidae (Coleoptera) in baited pitfall traps, segregated by bait.

ence. There was no significant difference in attractancy between the two killing-preservative agents used (graph 56), but there was a very significant difference (P < .001) in baits utilized, with fish much more attractive.

Family: Lagriidae

Lagriidae, or lagriid beetles, are elongate, dark-colored beetles of medium size (10 to 15 mm), which are closely related to Tenebrionidae and difficult to separate from it. Usually lagriids are separated from tenebrionids by the front coxal cavity, which is globose in Lagriidae, and the elongate last antennal segment in many species of Lagriidae (fig. 76). Adults and larvae have similar habits to Tenebrionidae, living under bark or in fallen tree trunks, where they feed on leaves and detritus.

Lagriidae is a relatively small family of less than 400 known

Graph 56.   Collections of Hydrophilidae (Coleoptera) in baited pitfall traps, segregated by preservatives.

species. In Reserva Ducke lagriids were not frequently encountered, but were collected in all traps, except baited pitfall traps. They were most often taken in the flight trap, where a total of 31 were collected. They appeared to be most frequently taken in March, but numbers were too small to be significant, and a few individuals were present throughout the study.

Family: Lampyridae

Lampyridae, or firefly beetles, are elongate, flattened beetles of medium size (5 to 20 mm) with 7 or 8 abdominal segments and head covered by the pronotum. Normally luminescent organs are present on the 6th or 7th sternites (fig. 77). Color and periodicity of luminescense varies between species. Larvae, like adults, can occasionally be luminescent. Larvae are predaceous, living on the moist forest floor among the detritus. A few larvae are aquatic. Adults apparently do not normally feed, although a few predaceous species feed on other fireflies,

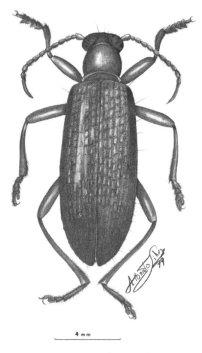

4 mm

Figure 76.   Lagriidae (Coleoptera).

Figure 77.   Lampyridae (Coleoptera).

attracting them by means of a similar luminescent flash pattern used in mating (Wickler 1968).

There are slightly over 1700 lampyrid species described. They are common in Reserva Ducke where they were found in all traps, except baited pitfall traps. Lampyrids were more than 6 times as frequent in 15 m light traps than at 1 m. They accounted for more than 1% of beetles in the flight trap. February to May seems to be the predominant emergence time (graph 57). Biomass of lampyrids was generally quite low.

Family: Languriidae

Languriidae, or lizard beetles, are elongate, cylindrical beetles of medium size (5 to 10 mm) with four tarsal segments on all legs (fig. 78). Larvae are stem borers while adults feed on pollen and leaves.

The family is a relatively small one, with about 450 described species. Languriids were not commonly encountered at Reserva Ducke, but two individuals were taken from 15 m light traps on 6 Sept. 1977.

142   *Insecta*

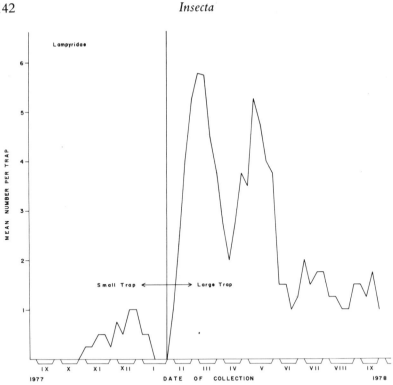

Graph 57.   Collections of Lampyridae (Coleoptera) in the flight trap.

Family: Lathridiidae

Lathridiidae, or minute brown scavenger beetles, are tiny (1 to 3 mm), brown, elongate beetles with three tarsal segments (fig. 79). Larvae and adults live on mold and decomposing plant materials.

There are about 520 described species of Lathridiidae. At Reserva Ducke they were encountered in low numbers in all types of traps, except the flight trap. Greatest numbers were encountered in the 15 m light traps (17) where they were most common in August and September.

Family: Leiodidae

Leiodidae, or round fungus beetles, are rounded, shiny dark beetles which are capable of rolling up into a ball (fig. 80). The Amazonian species have a 3- to 5-segmented antennal club with reduced eighth segment. This family is closely related to Leptodiridae, and indeed some specialists (Peck, personal communication) prefer to place the Leptodiridae within the Leiodidae as the subfamily Catopinae. They can be differentiated by the more elongate shape and inability of Leptodiridae to form a ball. Both adults and larvae of Leiodidae live on fungus and decaying vegetable matter.

Leiodidae is a small family with about 500 described species. A total of 138 individuals were taken in Reserva Ducke, principally in emergence (91) and baited pitfall traps (33). Both these trapping techniques indicated a low, but rather constant population level of Leiodidae throughout the year.

Family: Leptodiridae

Leptodiridae, or small carrion beetles, are small (2 to 5 mm), elongate, tapering beetles with depressed head (fig. 81). They have a characteristically small eighth antennal segment, and can be separated from the closely related Leiodidae by the more elongate shape and inability to roll into a ball. Members of this

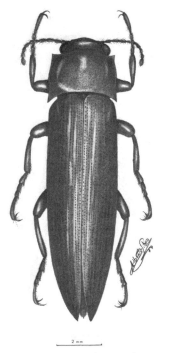

2 mm

Figure 78.   Languriidae (Coleoptera).

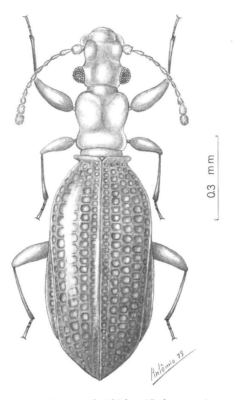

0.3 mm

Figure 79.   Lathridiidae (Coleoptera).

family are generally encountered associated with carrion or in mammal burrows, and occasionally in ant nests.

Leptodiridae is a rather small family with only about 600 described species. They are commonly encountered in Reserva Ducke, especially in the baited pitfall traps, with the population peak coming in mid-November, at the beginning of the rainy season (graph 58). As indicated in graph 59, the collecting pre- servative fluid made no significant difference in attractancy, but there was a very significant difference in attractancy between carrion and feces (graph 60). Although feces continued attract- ing leptodirids throughout the year, from late October until late March, the carrion attracted much larger quantities of in- dividuals. Altogether, 63% of the leptodirids in pitfall traps

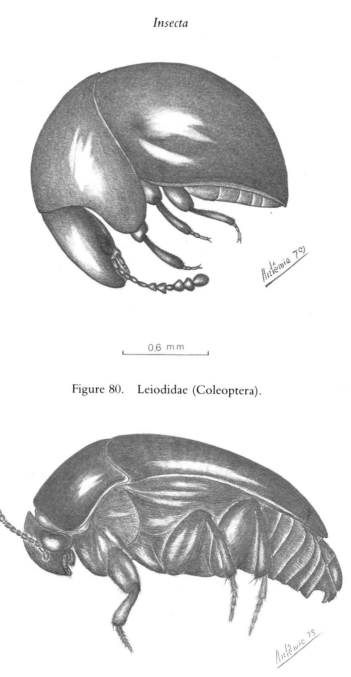

0.6 mm

Figure 80.　Leiodidae (Coleoptera).

0.6 mm

Figure 81.　Leptodiridae (Coleoptera).

came to carrion and 69% from mid–October until the end of March.

In terms of arthropod biomass, Leptodiridae contributed about 2% in baited pitfall traps. The small biomass in relation to numbers is a reflection primarily of the large size of some other groups, especially Scarabaeidae.

Family: Limnichidae

Limnichidae, or minute marsh-loving beetles, are small (1 to 2 mm), oval beetles with 10-segmented antennae, and relatively large claws (fig. 82). Both larvae and adults are aquatic.

Limnichidae is a very small family with only about 70 species described. Only one individual was encountered in Reserva

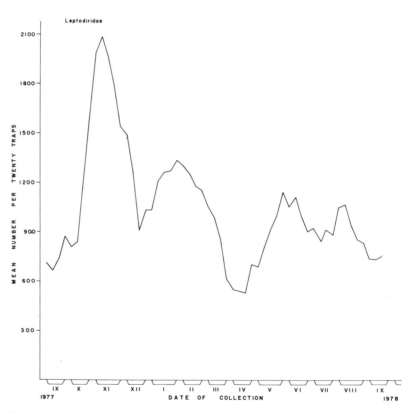

Graph 58.   Collections of Leptodiridae (Coleoptera) from baited pitfall traps.

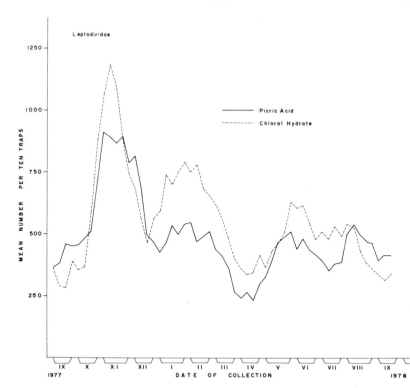

Graph 59.   Collections of Leptodiridae (Coleoptera) in baited pitfall traps, segregated by preservatives.

Ducke, in a 15 m light trap on 16 Aug. 1977 at the height of dry season.

Family: Lycidae

Lycidae, or lycid beetles, are medium-sized (5 to 18 mm) beetles with elytra less sclerotized than in most other families of beetles (fig. 83). They are closely related to Lampyridae, but can be separated from fireflies by the widely separated middle coxae. Larvae and adults are both predaceous, and this family is well-known for its mimicry complexes with cockroaches, grasshoppers, moths, and other beetle families (Wickler 1968).

Lycidae is a medium-sized family of more than 3000 described species. Lycids were frequently encountered at Reserva Ducke, especially in 15 m light traps and the flight trap. Lycids were more than 12 times as common at 15 m height as at 1 m. Data from light traps and the flight trap indicate no peak of emergence, but rather a steady population level throughout the year (graph 61).

Family: Lymexylonidae

Lymexylonidae, or ship timber beetles are unmistakable beetles of medium to large size (10 to 42 mm) with very elongate body, short antennae, and often short elytra or flabellate maxillary palpi (fig. 84). Larvae and adults feed on fungus in rotting wood, and occasionally attacked ship timbers in the days of sailing ships.

Lymexylonidae is a very small family with less than 50 described species worldwide. They are often split into two families, Lymexylonidae and Telegeusidae. They are much more common in tropical than temperate climates. In Reserva Ducke 12 individuals were taken from 15 m light traps (3) and the

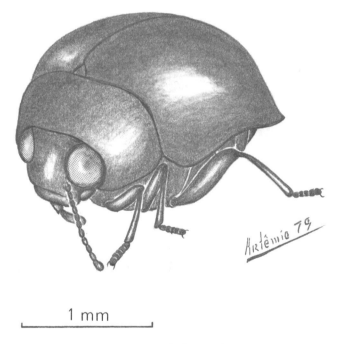

1 mm

Figure 82.   Limnichidae (Coleoptera).

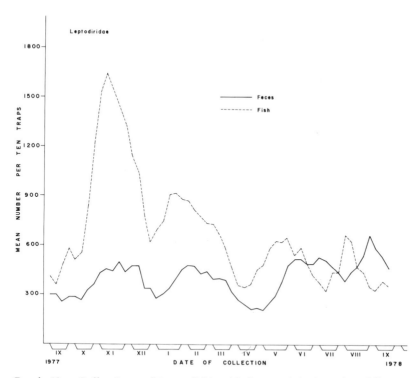

Graph 60. Collections of Leptodiridae (Coleoptera) in baited pitfall traps, segregated by bait.

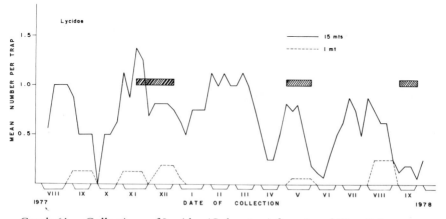

Graph 61. Collections of Lycidae (Coleoptera) from 1 and 15 m light traps.

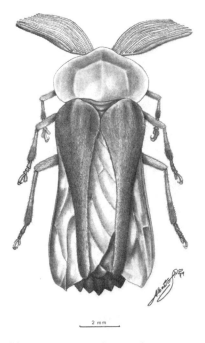

Figure 83.   Lycidae (Coleoptera).

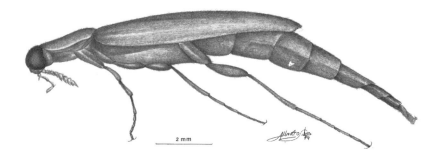

Figure 84.   Lymexylonidae (Coleoptera).

flight trap (9). The three lymexylonids from the light traps were taken on 15 Nov., 13 Dec., and 3 Jan. Those individuals taken from the flight trap were collected mainly in the months of February and March.

Family: Melandryidae

Melandryidae, or false darkling beetles, are medium-sized, elongate, tapering beetles with 5-5-4 tarsal formula (fig. 85). Larvae and adults live under bark or in wood, where some species are predaceous and others fungus feeders.

This is a relatively small family with less than 700 species described worldwide. Melandryidae were taken in all types of traps at Reserva Ducke, except baited pitfall traps, with the majority collected in the flight trap (70). Data from the flight trap indicate a rather low but constant population from February to September.

Family: Meloidae

Meloidae, or blister beetles, are small to large-sized (3 to 30 mm), elongate beetles with large head in proportion to prothorax and 5-5-4 tarsal formula (fig. 86). Some species have

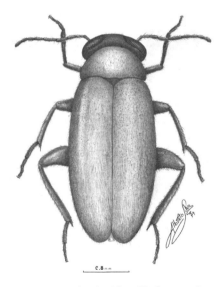

Figure 85.   Melandryidae (Coleoptera).

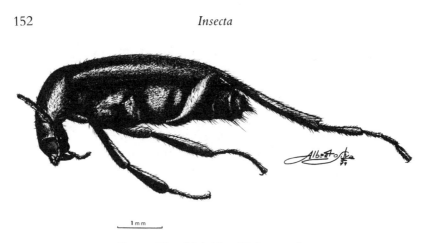

Figure 86.   Meloidae (Coleoptera).

short wings, others are long-winged. Larval meloids are parasitic on bees and grasshopper eggs. They are hypermeta-
morphic with an active "triungulin" 1st instar. Subsequent instars are sluggish and scarabaeiform, remaining close to the
host. Adults are phytophagous, generally seeking out solana-
ceous plants. Some species are pests of potatoes.

Adults produce an internal chemical substance called can-
tharidin, which when the body is crushed or roughly handled,
will cause a skin irritation and blistering. Hence, the common
name blister beetle. The "Spanish fly" which is said to have
aphrodisiac powers is the ground up bodies of one species of
Meloidae.

There are over 2000 known species of Meloidae, most commonly encountered in arid areas. One species of beetle was
taken in Reserva Ducke in light, flight and emergence traps,
which we have had difficulty in identifying to family. We think
that it is probably a meloid, and are here considering it as such.

Family: Monommidae

Monommidae, or monommid beetles, are small to medium-
sized (5 to 12 mm) shiny, dark, oval beetles with 5-5-4 tarsal
formula (fig. 87). Larvae live under rotten wood, and adults
are found in detritus.

This is a small family with about 200 described species worldwide. About 60 species are known from the Western Hemi-

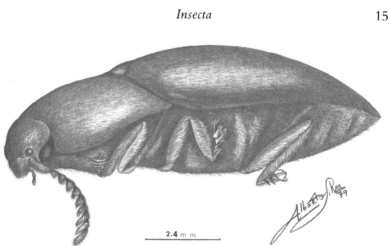

Figure 87.   Monommidae (Coleoptera).

sphere. Monommids were encountered in Reserva Ducke in all
types of traps, except baited pitfall traps. The vast majority
were collected in the flight trap, where they appeared in low
numbers from February to September.

Family: Mordellidae

Mordellidae, or tumbling flower beetles, are small to medium-
sized (1.5 to 15 mm), acutely tapering beetles with depressed

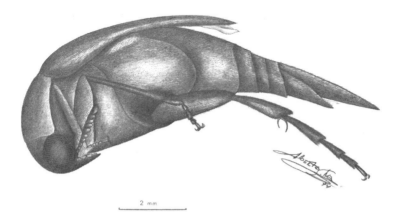

Figure 88.   Mordellidae (Coleoptera).

heads and long posterior legs (fig. 88). Larvae may be carnivorous, parasitic, or leaf miners. Adults are phytophagous.

There are about 700 known species of Mordellidae. They were collected in Reserva Ducke from all types of traps, except baited pitfall traps, but 97% were found in the flight trap. They were much more frequently collected in the flight trap during the height of the dry season in August and September (graph 62).

Family: Mycetophagidae

Mycetophagidae, or hairy fungus beetles, are small (1.5 to 6 mm), hairy, rounded beetles with 3-4-4-, or 4-4-4- or 5-5-5-tarsal formula (fig. 89). Both larvae and adults feed on fungus.

There are a little more than 200 described species of Mycetophagidae known. They were occasionally found in all types of traps at Reserva Ducke, except baited pitfall traps. A little more than half were taken from 15 m light traps. They were collected most frequently from light traps from September to December, or the beginning of the rainy season.

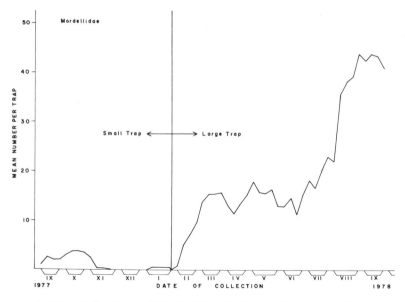

Graph 62.   Collections of Mordellidae (Coleoptera) from the flight trap.

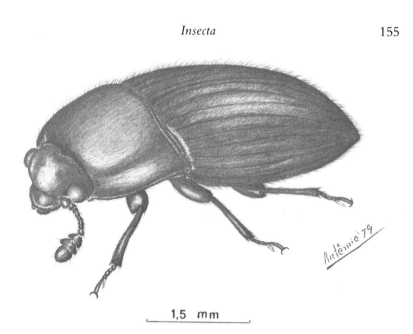

Figure 89.   Mycetophagidae (Coleoptera).

Family: Nilionidae

Nilionidae are a small group of beetles (fig. 90) confined to the Neotropical Region. They are medium-sized (7 to 11 mm), rounded beetles with head located ventrally below wide, strap-like pronotum. They have 5-5-4 tarsal formula and elytra sharply angled laterally, so that part of the elytra appears to be a ventral extension of the body.

In Reserva Ducke these insects have been infrequently collected. However, none were collected during the study.

Family: Nitidulidae

Nitidulidae, or sap beetles, are small (1.5 to 5 mm), oval beetles with three-segmented antennal club and transverse anterior coxal cavity (fig. 91). Larvae and adults of Nitidulidae as a family are quite variable from plant feeders, to fungus feeders, to sap feeders, to predators. The majority of species feed on fermenting plant parts.

Nitidulidae is a fairly large family with close to 2300 described species. In Reserva Ducke, Nitidulidae was a commonly encountered family in all types of traps, especially flight, emergence, and baited pitfall traps.

In the baited pitfall traps, there appeared to be three distinct population peaks in late October, March, and August (graph 63). As shown in graph 64, the October and August peaks seemed to be associated with picric acid traps, while the March peak was associated with chloral hydrate traps. This could be due to differences in species of Nitidulidae involved.

Family: Nosodendridae

Nosodendridae, or nosodendrid beetles, are small (4 to 6 mm), dark, oval beetles with mentum that completely covers the mouth (fig. 92). Larvae and adults live in rotten wood and under bark where they are probably predaceous on dipterous larvae.

Nosodendridae is a very small family of only about 30 known species. Only one nosodendrid was found at Reserva Ducke, in an emergence trap on 10 Jan.

5 mm

Figure 90.   Nilionidae (Coleoptera).

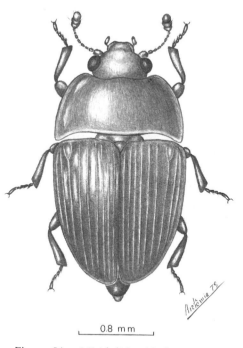

Figure 91. Nitidulidae (Coleoptera).

Family: Noteridae

Noteridae, or burrowing water beetles, are small (1.2 to 5.5 mm), streamlined aquatic beetles which closely resemble Dytiscidae, except that the scutellum is covered by the elytra in Noteridae (fig. 93). Larvae and adults are aquatic, feeding on other aquatic insects.

Noteridae is a small family of about 150 species. One individual was collected in Reserva Ducke in an emergence trap on 30 May. No good explanation could be found for its presence there.

Family: Oedemeridae

Oedemeridae, or false blister beetles, are elongate beetles of medium size (5 to 20 mm) with 5-5-4 tarsal formula and a pronotum which is widest at its anterior margin (fig. 94). Larvae live in moist, decaying wood and adults feed on nectar and pollen.

This family is mostly tropical and subtropical in distribution, with about 1500 species known. In Reserva Ducke they were collected in 15 m light traps, flight traps, and emergence traps. Both light trap and flight trap data indicate a sharp August–October emergence peak, during the height of the dry season.

Family: Orthoperidae

Orthoperidae, or minute fungus beetles, are very small (.5 to 5 mm) oval beetles with pronotum completely covering the head (fig. 95). Adults live as carnivores in moist, rotting wood.

This family, sometimes called Corylophidae, contains about 300 known species. In Reserva Ducke they were collected in light traps, emergence traps and baited pitfall traps, but over

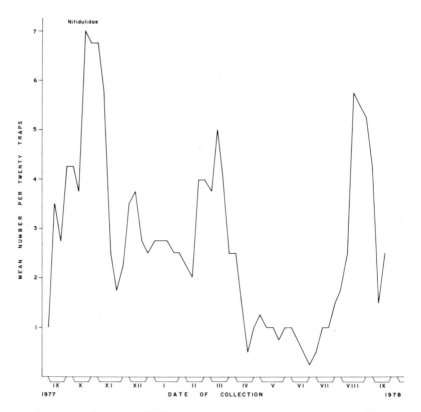

Graph 63.   Collections of Nitidulidae (Coleoptera) from baited pitfall traps.

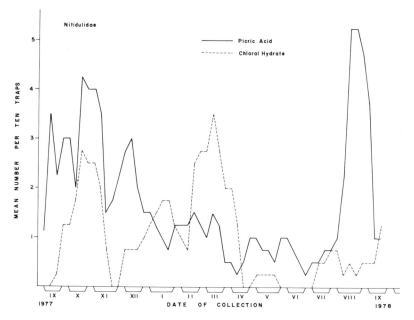

Graph 64. Collections of Nitidulidae (Coleoptera) from baited pitfall traps, segregated by preservatives.

70% of them were in 15 m light traps. Data from the light traps indicate a broad emergence during the rainy season from mid-November until March (graph 65).

Family: Ostomidae

Ostomidae, or bark-gnawing beetles, are medium-sized to large (6 to 50 mm) elongate, flattened, dark-colored beetles with prominent mandibles and pronotum separated from elytra (fig. 96). Larvae may be carnivorous on insects in rotting wood or phytophagous on stored grains or fungi.

There are about 600 known species in the family, sometimes known as Trogossitidae. In Amazonia, one species, *Temnoscheila colossus* Serville, reaches a length of 50 mm. In Reserva Ducke, only four individuals were encountered: one in a 1 m light trap on 6 Sept. 1977; two in the flight trap on 28 Feb. and 30 May; and one in an emergence trap on 22 Nov.

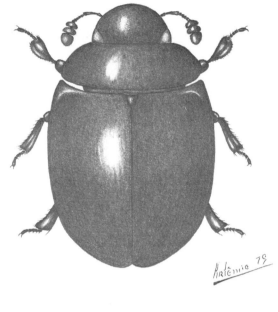

1,2 mm

Figure 92.   Nosodendridae (Coleoptera).

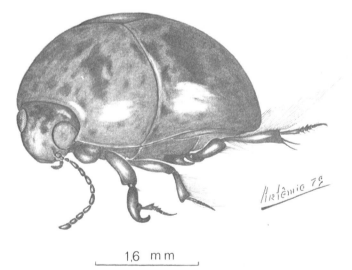

1,6 mm

Figure 93.   Noteridae (Coleoptera).

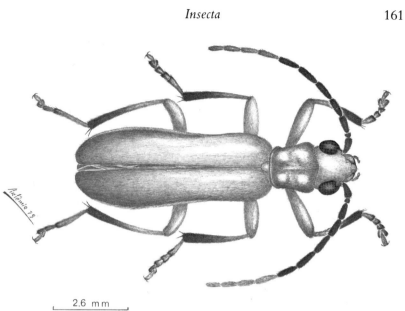

Figure 94.   Oedemeridae (Coleoptera).

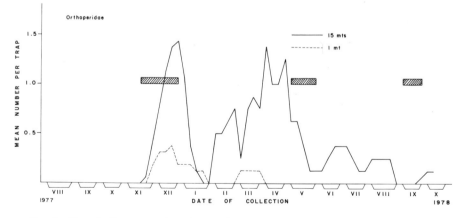

Graph 65.   Collections of Orthoperidae (Coleoptera) from 1 and 15 m light
traps.

Family: Passalidae

Passalidae, or bess beetles, are large (30 to 40 mm) elongate beetles with sublamellate antennae and characteristic quadrate pronotum (fig. 97). Adults and larvae live in colonies in decayed wood, where they communicate with one another by stridulations.

There are about 500 described species, almost all of which are tropical in distribution. Only two passalids were taken in traps at Reserva Ducke, both in 15 m light traps on 6 Dec. and 14 March. They were *Popilus marginatus* Percheron.

Family: Pedilidae

Pedilidae, or false ant-like flower beetles, are medium-sized (7 to 12 mm), elongate beetles with a constriction behind the head

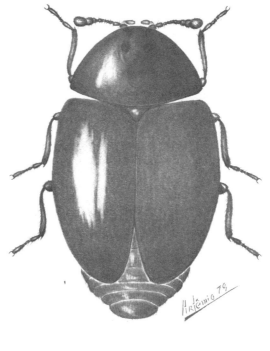

0,5 mm

Figure 95.   Orthoperidae (Coleoptera).

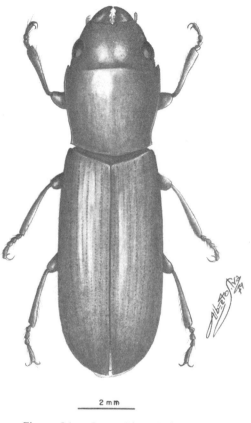

Figure 96. Ostomidae (Coleoptera).

and 5-5-4 tarsal formula (fig. 98). They are similar to Anthicidae but can be separated from the latter group by larger size and oval to emarginate compound eyes. Larvae live in detritus on the forest floor, while adults are encountered on leaves and flowers.

There are about 250 known species of Pedilidae worldwide. In Reserva Ducke four pedilids were encountered: two in the flight trap on 11 and 18 April and two in emergence traps on 10 Jan. and 7 March.

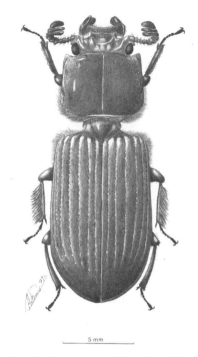

5 mm

Figure 97.   *Passalus rhodocanthopoides*, Passalidae (Coleoptera).

Family: Phalacridae

Phalacridae, or shining flower beetles, are small (1 to 3 mm), rounded beetles with 4-4-4- tarsal formula (fig. 99). Larvae live in flowers, or sometimes under bark.

Phalacridae is a small family of about 500 described species. Only eight individuals were caught at Reserva Ducke—seven of them in 15 m light traps. All phalacrids from light traps were collected on three dates: 16 Aug. 1977, 23 Aug. 1977, and 15 Nov. The one individual in an emergence trap was taken on 28 March.

Family: Phengodidae

Phengodidae, or glowworms, are characterized by striking dimorphism between the sexes. Females are larviform and very similar to phengodid larvae. Males are short-winged, with plu–

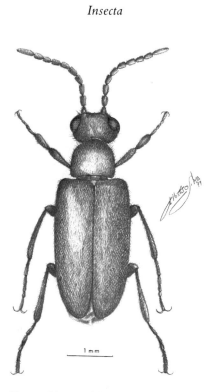

Figure 98.   Pedilidae (Coleoptera).

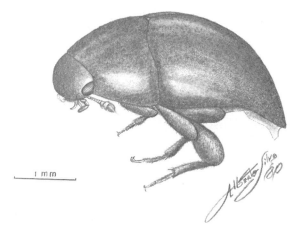

Figure 99.   Phalacridae (Coleoptera).

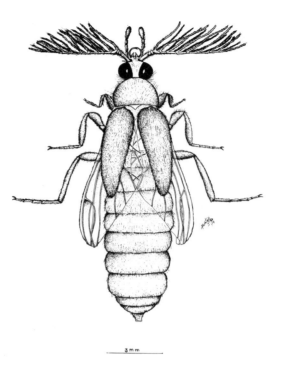

Figure 100.   Phengodidae (Coleoptera).

mose antennae and prominent mandibles (fig. 100). Larvae are luminescent, living as predators on other soft-bodied arthropods on the forest floor. Size of adult males varies from 5 to 30 mm in length.

There are only 56 known species of Phengodidae, all from the Americas. This family was encountered in 1 m light traps (but not 15 m light traps), and emergence traps, although 88% were found in the flight trap. Data from the flight trap indicate low and rather constant population levels from February through September.

Family: Platypodidae

Platypodidae, or pinhole borers, are elongate, cylindrical beetles of small to medium size (2 to 8 mm), which are closely related to Scolytidae, but can be quickly separated from the latter family by the very elongate first tarsal segment (fig. 101). Larvae and

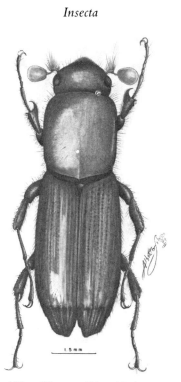

Figure 101.   Platypodidae (Coleoptera).

adults live in galleries in trees formed by the adults. Larvae feed on fungus.

Platypodidae is a medium-sized family with about 1000 described species, mainly tropical. In Reserva Ducke 470 individuals were collected from all types of traps, except baited pitfall traps. Data from 15 m light traps indicates an early December emergence peak (graph 66).

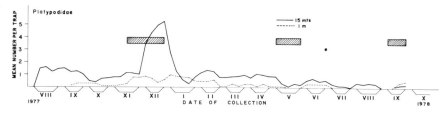

Graph 66.   Collections of Platypodidae (Coleoptera) from 1 and 15 m light traps.

Family: Pselaphidae

Pselaphidae, or short-winged mold beetles, are small (0.5 to 5.5 mm), short-winged beetles which live in the soil and leaf litter (fig. 102). They are similar to Staphylinidae, but generally have more clubbed antennae, stouter appearance and smaller size. Some species are remarkably good ant mimics. Most species are free-living on mold in the forest, but some are ant and mammal nest associates, while others are cave-dwellers.

Pselaphidae is a large family of about 5000 described species. Pselaphids were encountered in all types of traps at Reserva Ducke, especially emergence traps, where they accounted for almost 4% of all beetles collected. Short-winged mold beetles were more than twice as common in 1 m light traps as 15 m light traps. Populations never reached very high levels in any of the traps, but they were continuously present throughout the year (graph 67).

Family: Ptiliidae

Ptiliidae, or feather-winged beetles are minute (.25 to 1.0 mm) beetles of oval shape and characteristic narrow hingwings with

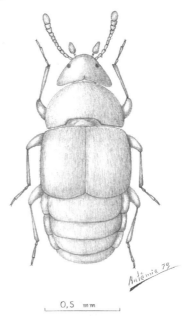

0,5 mm

Figure 102.   Pselaphidae (Coleoptera).

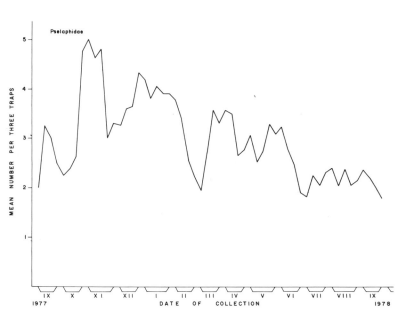

Graph 67. Collections of Pselaphidae (Coleoptera) from the emergence
traps.

a dense fringe of long hairs, giving the wings the appearance
of feathers (fig. 103). The family includes the smallest of beetles,
living on fungal spores on the forest floor, in rotten logs, be-
neath bark, and other moist places conducive to fungal growth.

There are about 300 known species of Ptiliidae. In Reserva
Ducke they were encountered in emergence traps, but more
than 98% were found in the baited pitfall traps, making them
the third most commonly encountered beetle family during the
study. There appeared to be two seasonal peaks in population
growth, the first occurring in August (graph 68). We find that
with this family both bait and killing-preservative fluid influence pitfall trap captures (P < .001). Graph 69 demonstrates the
preference of ptiliids for picric acid over chloral hydrate, while
graph 70 shows the preference for feces over carrion. Obviously, maximal attractancy was achieved using traps with
picric acid and feces. Because of their small size, ptiliid biomass
was insignificant.

Family: Ptilodactylidae

Ptilodactylidae, or toed-winged beetles, are medium-sized (5 to 6 mm) insects very similar to Chrysomelidae, except for the depressed head and partially expanded pronotum (fig. 104). Males have basal processes on antennal segments 4 to 10. Larvae live in moist, decaying wood or are aquatic. Adults are found resting on herbaceous vegetation near water.

Ptilodactylidae is a small family of less than 200 known species. They were commonly encountered in traps at Reserva Ducke, except for baited pitfall traps. They accounted for almost 3% of all beetles entering the flight trap. There was a definite population peak during August–September 1978, but this was not noted in September 1977.

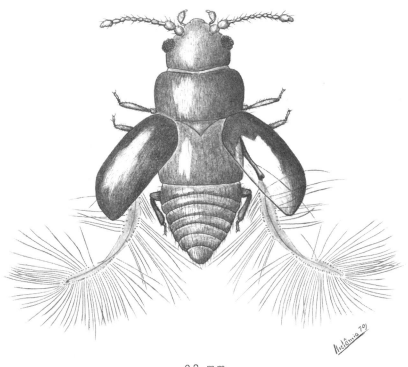

0.2 mm

Figure 103.   Ptiliidae (Coleoptera).

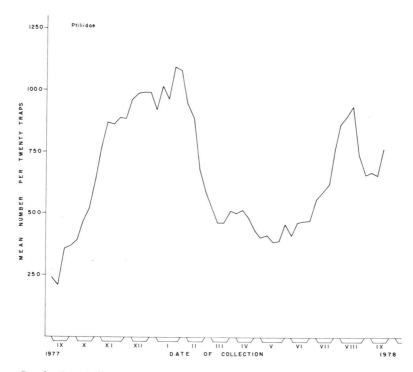

Graph 68. Collections of Ptiliidae (Coleoptera) from baited pitfall traps.

Family: Rhipiceridae

Rhipiceridae, or cedar beetles, are large (16 to 20 mm), elongate, dark beetles with lamellate antennae (fig. 105). Larvae and adults generally feed on rotten wood.

Rhipiceridae is a small family of 180 known species. In Reserva Ducke this family was seldom encountered, with 10 individuals taken from the flight trap and one from the emergence trap. The majority of specimens were collected in October and November.

Family: Rhipiphoridae

Rhipiphoridae, or rhipiphorid beetles, are elongate beetles of medium size (4 to 15 mm). Males have pectinate and females serrate antennae. Among known rhipiphorids from Reserva Ducke, all are short-winged. Eyes are extremely large, practically covering the head (fig. 106). Larvae are parasitic on bees,

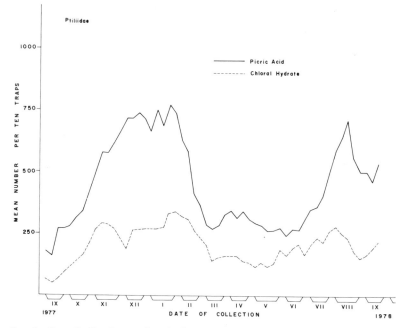

Graph 69.   Collections of Ptiliidae (Coleoptera) from baited pitfall traps, segregated by preservatives.

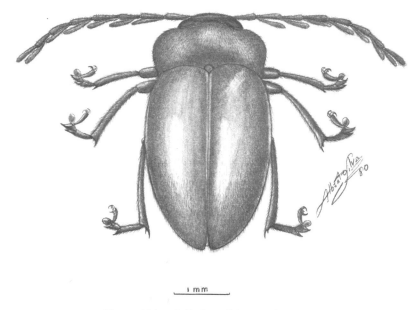

Figure 104.   Ptilodactylidae (Coleoptera).

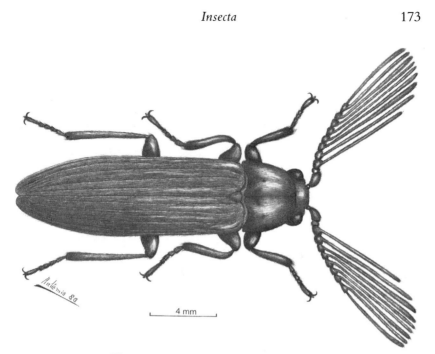

Figure 105. Rhipiceridae (Coleoptera).

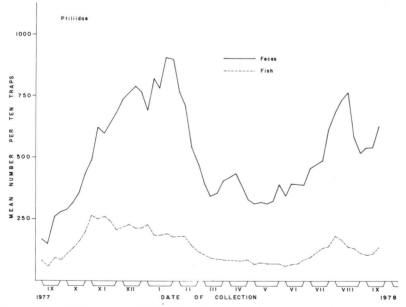

Graph 70. Collections of Ptiliidae (Coleoptera) from baited pitfall traps, segregated by baits.

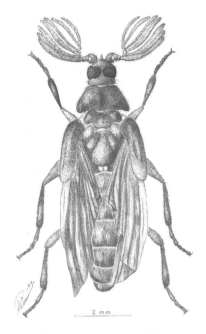

Figure 106.   Rhipiphoridae (Coleoptera).

wasps and cockroaches. First instar larvae are active in seeking out hosts. Subsequent instars are scarabaeiform. Initially the larvae live internally, but later may live externally.

Fewer than 300 species have been described worldwide. In Reserva Ducke 13 individuals were found in 1 m light traps (3) and the flight trap (10). Collection dates were scattered between March and mid-October.

Family: Rhizophagidae

Rhizophagidae, or root-eating beetles, are small (1.5 to 3 mm), cylindrical beetles with two-segmented antennal club and elytra not completely covering the abdomen (fig. 107). Larvae and adults are predaceous, living in rotten wood, under bark or in tunnels of wood-boring beetles.

Rhizophagidae is a small family with only about 200 described species. In Reserva Ducke Rhizophagidae was very seldom encountered. One individual was taken from the flight trap and nine other rhizophagids were found in emergence traps.

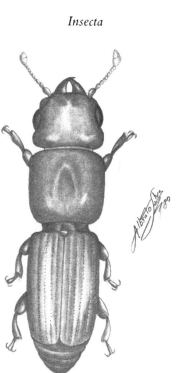

Figure 107. Rhizophagidae (Coleoptera).

Family: Salpingidae

Salpingidae, or narrow-waisted bark beetles, are medium-sized (2 to 15 mm), dark beetles with open precoxal cavities, subquadrate pronotum, and 5-5-4 tarsal formula (fig. 108). They are carnivorous as both larvae and adults, living under bark and in rotten wood.

There are about 300 described species of Salpingidae, mainly in tropical areas. Only eight salpingids were found in Reserva Ducke, in 1 m light traps (1), 15 m light traps (3) and the flight trap (4). These eight individuals were taken during scattered intervals throughout the year.

Family: Scaphidiidae

Scaphidiidae, or shining fungus beetles, are small to medium-sized (2 to 7 mm), shiny, oval beetles with truncate elytra not covering the last abdominal segments (fig. 109). Larvae and adults feed on fungus in rotting wood and under bark.

Scaphidiidae is a small family with only about 300 described species. They were found in Reserva Ducke in all types of traps, except 1 m light traps, although the majority were collected from the flight trap. They can be collected throughout the year, but populations appear to be highest from March to May (graph 71).

Family: Scarabaeidae
Scarabaeidae, or scarab beetles, are small to large (2 to 160 mm), rounded beetles with lamellate antennae (fig. 110). Some of the world's largest and most brightly colored beetles are found in this family, making them a very popular group of insects. In the central Amazon Basin, *Megasoma acteon* and *Megasoma mars* are among the largest of beetles, almost covering the palm of

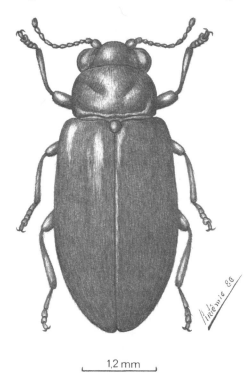

1,2 mm

Figure 108.   Salpingidae (Coleoptera).

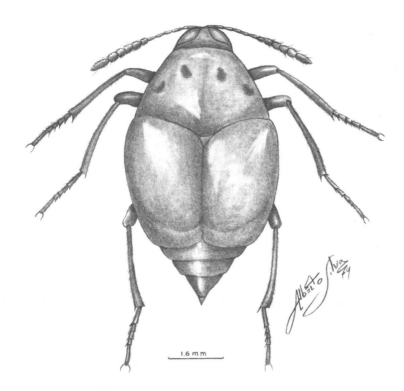

Figure 109.   Scaphidiidae (Coleoptera).

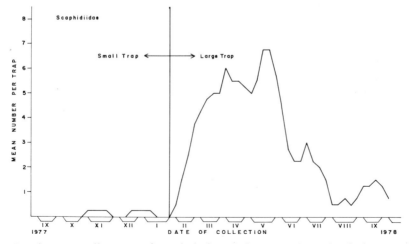

Graph 71.   Collections of Scaphidiidae (Coleoptera) from the flight trap.

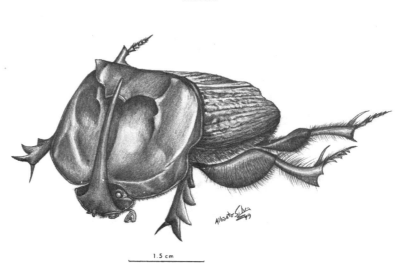

1.5 cm

Figure 110.   Scarabaeidae (Coleoptera).

a person's hand. The prominent horn of males of these species are often used in the Manaus area as necklace ornaments.

Larvae feed on plant roots, rotting logs, carrion or feces, in the latter case, often in characteristically formed balls. Adults of Rutelinae feed on leaves and fruit of plants, sometimes causing extensive damage to local fruit crops. Some species of Troginae are associated with mammal burrows. Other groups are associated with termites, pollen, sap, carrion and fungus.

Scarabaeidae is a large family with about 20,000 described species. In Reserva Ducke scarabs were found in all types of traps, but more than 98% were taken from baited pitfall traps. Within these pitfall traps they constituted the fourth most common family of beetles (9%), and between 63 and 95% of all arthropod biomass within these traps. Because of their large size and heavy sclerotization, their dry weight (biomass) far surpassed all other groups encountered in the study, and they have to be considered as one of the primary sources of animal biomass within the Neotropical forest ecosystem, although their contribution is often masked by the narrow habitat preference (feces, for example) of many species.

Populations of scarabs remained high throughout the year, although there appeared to be a major emergence peak in January–February, and secondary peaks in June and September (graph 72). Scarabaeidae, like Ptiliidae, demonstrates that both bait and killing-preservative fluid are statistically significant (P < .001) in attractancy. Graph 73 shows the preference for feces over fish, and graph 74 demonstrates the preference for picric acid over chloral hydrate. Relatively few scarabs were caught in the light traps. It is interesting to note (graph 75) that more were attracted to light at the 1 m level, even though a few scarabs were caught at 15 m. This is one of the few families which showed more activity at ground level than in the canopy.

Family: Scolytidae

Scolytidae, or bark beetles, are small (1 to 9 mm), dark, cylindrical beetles with geniculate antennae (fig. 111). They are similar to Cisidae and Platypodidae, but can be separated from the former by the geniculate antennae, and from the latter by the first tarsal segment not being longer than the subsequent four segments. Larvae are phytophagous, living in seeds, stems, roots, etc. The majority attack wood, where they can cause

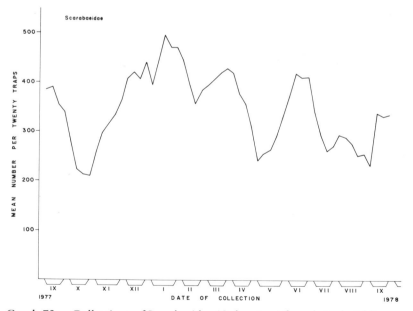

Graph 72.   Collections of Scarabaeidae (Coleoptera) from baited pitfall traps.

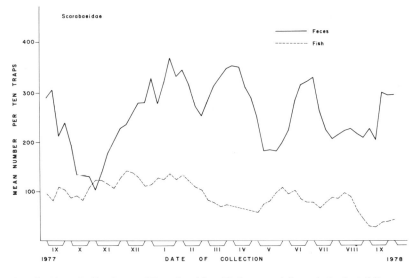

Graph 73.   Collections of Scarabaeidae (Coleoptera) from baited pitfall traps,
            segregated by bait.

considerable damage just below the bark, or they can be vectors
of plant diseases, creating complete deforestation of some areas,
as with the Dutch Elm Disease of eastern North America.

Scolytidae is a large family of 6000 to 7000 known species.
Scolytids were common in all types of traps in Reserva Ducke,

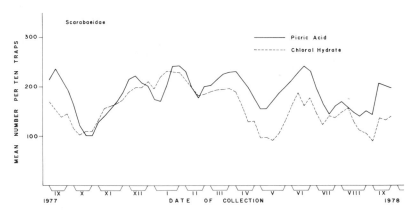

Graph 74.   Collections of Scarabaeidae (Coleoptera) from baited pitfall traps,
            segregated by preservatives.

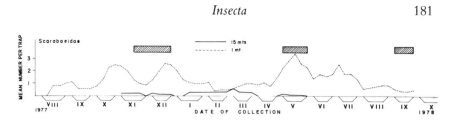

Graph 75.   Collections of Scarabaeidae (Coleoptera) from 1 and 15 m light
traps.

especially in emergence traps where they accounted for more
than 63% of all beetles collected. They were abundant enough
to generally make up 6.5% of all beetles in all traps. By dry
weight, Scolytidae was the dominant group of all arthropods
in emergence traps with a total of 20% of the biomass. Data
from the emergence traps indicate population emergence peaks
in January and again in April (graph 76). Baited pitfall trap data
shows the same January peak, but no April peak, as do light
traps (graph 79). However, a much stronger peak in baited

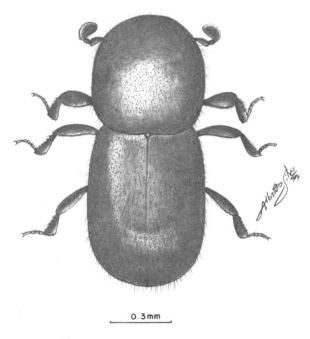

0.3 mm

Figure 111.   Scolytidae (Coleoptera).

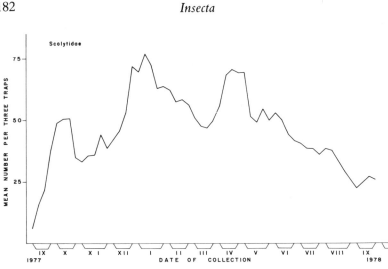

Graph 76.   Collections of Scolytidae (Coleoptera) from emergence traps.

pitfall traps is indicated for September–October (graph 77), which showed up only weakly in emergence trap results, and a smaller peak in November. Graph 78 shows that emergence peaks in November and January occurred almost solely in picric acid traps, while the stronger September peak occurred in all baited pitfall traps. Further study of the individual species involved may help elucidate more information on biology and behavior of this family and help explain why population peaks occurred as they did.

Family: Scydmaenidae

Scydmaenidae, or ant-like stone beetles, are small (1 to 5 mm), elongate beetles with generally swollen femur apices and ant-like appearance (fig. 112). Larvae and adults live in leaf litter, moss, or other moist woodland habitats. They appear to be mite predators.

Scydmaenidae is a medium-sized family with about 1200 described species. In Reserva Ducke they were found in all types of traps, but primarily in emergence traps where they accounted for almost 6% of all beetles. Emergence trap data indicates a major emergence peak in September, with a secondary peak in late March and early April (graph 80). Light trap data indicate an emergence in September and October (graph 81).

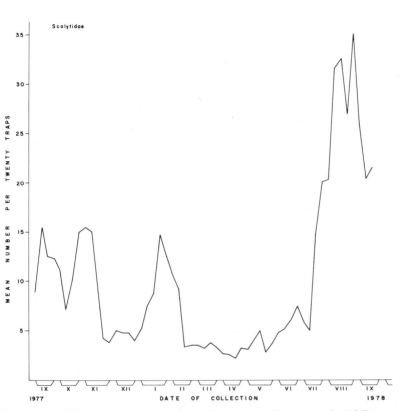

Graph 77.   Collections of Scolytidae (Coleoptera) from baited pitfall traps.

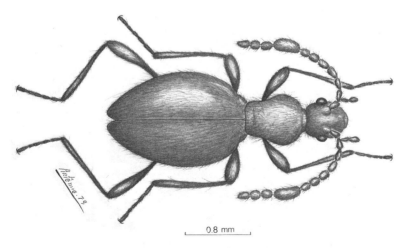

Figure 112.   Scydmaenidae (Coleoptera).

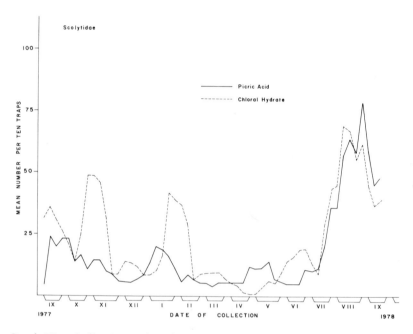

Graph 78.   Collections of Scolytidae (Coleoptera) from baited pitfall traps,
            segregated by preservatives.

Family: Staphylinidae

Staphylinidae, or rove beetles, are small to medium sized (1 to
20 mm), elongate beetles with clavate antennae and short wings
(fig. 113). Most larvae and adults of Staphylinidae occur in
detritus, under rocks, or bark, or in the soil where they feed
on decaying plant material, or are predaceous. Some forms are
ant and termite nest associates, while some other forms dwell
in caves.

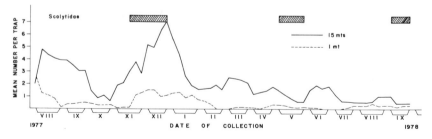

Graph 79.   Collections of Scolytidae (Coleoptera) from 1 and 15 m light
            traps.

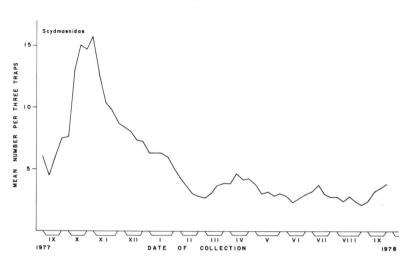

Graph 80. Collections of Scydmaenidae (Coleoptera) from emergence traps.

The family is very large with more than 27,000 species described. Rove beetles are found in almost .all tropical habitats, and were the dominant family of beetles encountered at Reserva Ducke, in terms of numbers. 56% of beetles in the 15 m light traps and 44% of beetles in the baited pitfall traps were Staphylinidae. Altogether, 40% of all beetles collected were Staphylinidae. However, because of their small size, they never accounted for more than 2% of all arthropod biomass in any traps, including baited pitfall traps.

Light trap data indicates a very dramatic emergence of Staphylinidae at the beginning of the rainy season in late November (graph 82) in the 15 m light traps, while no peak occurred at 1 m. This same dramatic peak is indicated from emergence trap

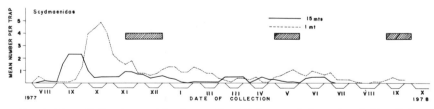

Graph 81. Collections of Scydmaenidae (Coleoptera) from 1 and 15 m light traps.

Insecta

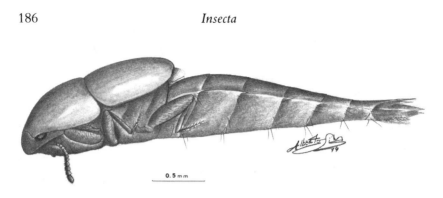

Figure 113.   Staphylinidae (Coleoptera).

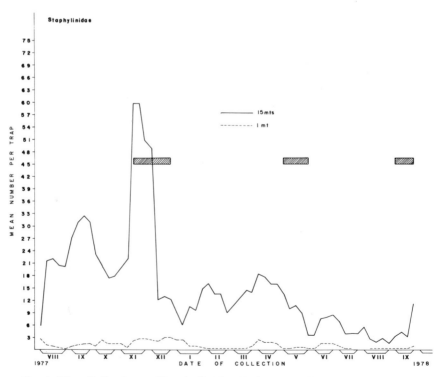

Graph 82.   Collections of Staphylinidae (Coleoptera) from 1 and 15 m light
traps.

data (graph 83), with secondary peaks in March and May. Finally, the baited pitfall traps also show an emergence peak in November, and an even stronger emergence peak in mid-January and a secondary peak in August (graph 84). Pitfall traps baited with feces were more attractive (P < .001) than fish (graph 85), and traps utilizing chloral hydrate were more attractive (P < .001) than picric acid.

On three occasions one emergence trap suddenly showed a large increase in population level, indicating a sudden emergence of many adult staphylinids from an area of 1 m², or less. As we have not heard of rove beetles congregating, or any type of social or subsocial organization, we find it difficult to explain why the sudden emergence in these isolated traps.

Family: Tenebrionidae

Tenebrionidae, or darkling beetles, are small to large (2 to 35 mm), elongate, dark beetles with 5-5-4 tarsal segmentation and first three abdominal sternites fused (fig. 114). They are very

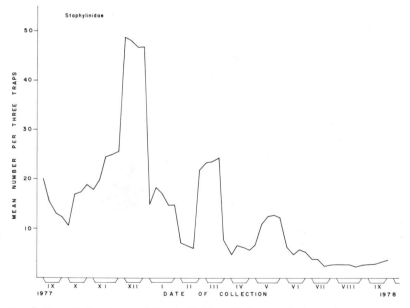

Graph 83. Collections of Staphylinidae (Coleoptera) from the emergence traps.

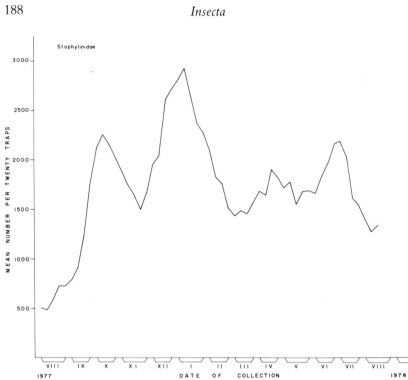

Graph 84.   Collections of Staphylinidae (Coleoptera) from baited pitfall traps.

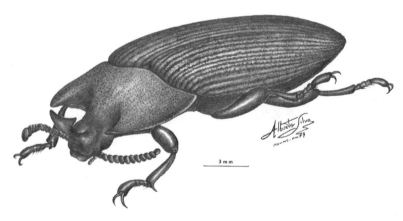

Figure 114.   Tenebrionidae (Coleoptera).

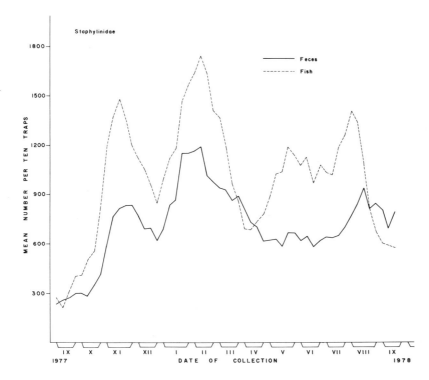

Graph 85. Collections of Staphylinidae (Coleoptera) from baited pitfall traps, segregated by baits.

similar to Lagriidae, but generally lack the elongate terminal segment and metallic coloration. Larvae and adults are scavengers on the forest floor, under leaves, in rotten wood and under stones. Some species have become associates of ant and termite nests.

Tenebrionidae is the fifth largest beetle family with about 15,000 known species. In traps at Reserva Ducke, tenebrionids were occasionally encountered, but only emergence traps yielded any significant numbers (89). Most tenebrionids in the emergence traps were caught in November and December (graph 86).

Family: Throscidae

Throscidae, or throscid beetles, are small (2 to 5 mm), oval beetles with recessed head and loose, three-segmented antennal

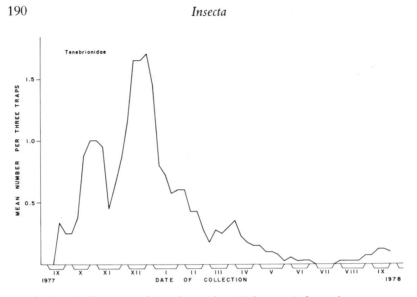

Graph 86.   Collections of Tenebrionidae (Coleoptera) from the emergence
            traps.

club (fig. 115). They appear similar to Anobiidae, but with a
more elongate shape and more prominent precoxae. Larvae live
in rotten wood and adults are found in flowers.

   Throscidae is a small family of about 200 species. Throscids
were occasionally collected in all types of traps at Reserva
Ducke, except baited pitfall traps, but were never very numerous.

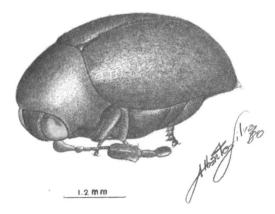

Figure 115.   Throscidae (Coleoptera).

ORDER: STREPSIPTERA

Strepsiptera, or twisted-winged insects, are a group of small insects characterized by very different habits and appearance between males and females. Males are 0.5 to 4 mm in length; with bulging eyes; antennae with elongate processes; short, heavily sclerotized forewings; and fan-shaped hindwings (fig. 116). Females are wingless, legless, eyeless larviform adults. She will never leave the host, but rather retain fertilized eggs within her body. Later she will give birth to between 1000 and 5000 first instar larvae. When the eggs hatch, the active larvae finds his way to the exterior and seeks the larva or nymph of a new host. Males upon emergence also seek to escape the host's body cavity, whereupon they seek out and mate with females which remain within the host. Adult males do not feed and probably live no more than one day.

Strepsiptera is one of the smallest orders of insects with about 350 known species. In Reserva Ducke, strepsipterans were encountered in both 1 m and 15 m light traps. Altogether, 56

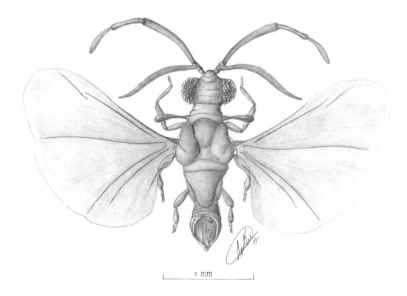

Figure 116.   Strepsiptera.

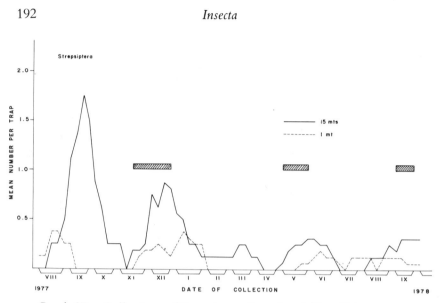

Graph 87.   Collections of Strepsiptera from 1 and 15 m light traps.

male strepsipterans were collected, with almost 3 times as many individuals from the 15 m traps as the 1 m traps. Strepsipterans were collected much more commonly during August to January (graph 87).

ORDER: MECOPTERA

Mecoptera, or scorpion flies, are an ancient assemblage of about 23 families, of which only nine exist today. During the early Permian, mecopterans were the second most common group of insects after cockroaches in some localities. In early Permian limestone deposits of central Kansas, scorpion-flies make up 40% of the fossil remains (Carpenter 1930). They are characterized by a simple holometabolous venation without a forked posterior cubital vein (CuP) and generally without extensive cross-veins (Meropeidae and Notiothaumidae are exceptions). Many of the more recent groups have the mouth-parts extended into an elongate rostrum.

Larvae may be phytophagous on moss (Boreidae, and probably Apteropanorpidae), on plant roots (Panorpodidae), saprophagous (Panorpidae and Bittacidae), or aquatic predators (Nannochoristidae). Adults may be predatory (Bittacidae), feed on leaf chlorophyll (Panorpodidae), or moss (Boreidae).

Mecoptera is today one of the smallest insectan orders, with 472 described species (Penny & Byers 1979). Three families are found in South America, but only one of these, Bittacidae (fig. 117), occurs in tropical areas. To date, only four bittacid species have been recorded from the Amazon Basin: *Nannobittacus elegans* (Esben-Petersen 1927), *Neobittacus aripuanaensis* (Penny 1977), *Pazius ornaticaudus* (Penny 1977), and a species of *Issikiella* (Penny & Byers, in preparation). Within Reserva Ducke, bittacids were collected from 1 m light traps on 15 and 22 Nov. and from the flight trap on 21 Feb., 14 and 28 March. These data tend to indicate a rainy season emergence for adult bittacids, and other collections within Amazonia tend to reinforce these conclusions, although isolated collections have been made throughout the year in the Manaus area.

ORDER: TRICHOPTERA
Trichoptera, or caddisflies, are a group of small to medium-sized insects which resemble small moths with long antennae.

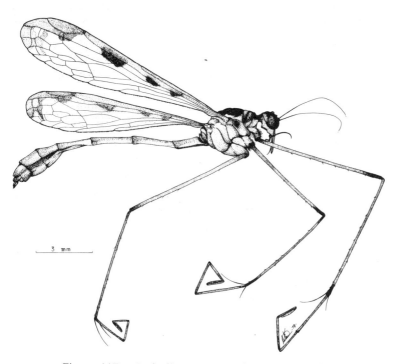

Figure 117. *Issikiella* sp., Bittacidae (Mecoptera).

They are often hairy, and in the central Amazon Basin many species have brightly colored scales on the wings. Larvae are aquatic, forming silken nets or free-living almost completely encapsulated within a case made of small pebbles, twigs, or leaf fragments. The case design is species or genus specific. Adults feed on liquids and often come to lights in large numbers (especially females) where they are easily recognized by their quick, jerky movements.

Trichoptera is a fairly large order with more than 5000 described species. There has been much recent work done on this group in northern South America. In nearby Surinam, Flint (1974) listed 10 families, 29 genera, and 124 species of Trichoptera and speculated that that number would eventually double. Flint has also treated five families of Trichoptera from the Amazon Basin. In the first work (Flint 1971) he treats the families Rhyacophilidae, Glossomatidae, Philopotamidae and Psychomyiidae with a total of 9 genera and 55 species. In the second paper (Flint 1978) he treats the family Hydropsychidae with 8 genera and 55 species. With the future addition of revisions within the remaining families, the Trichoptera probably are presently known from around 150 species within the Amazon Basin.

Within our terra firme study site at Reserva Ducke, trichopterans were not very common, being occasionally found in light and flight traps. During the weeks of total counts, an average of 4.3 trichopterans were found in the flight trap and nothing in the light traps. By far the most common species of Trichoptera in the flight trap was *Phyllocius fenestratus* Flint (fig. 118).

ORDER: LEPIDOPTERA

Lepidoptera, or butterflies, skippers, and moths, are a group well known to everyone. Holometabolous insects with brightly colored wings formed by millions of overlapping scales (fig. 119), these insects are readily visible in open areas in the tropical forest. Some butterflies, like the colorful *Morpho*, are also highly visible deep within the forest, although others, like the Satyridae have very drab coloration, or like glass-wings (*Cithaerias*), have no coloration at all. Adults are nectar feeders while larvae are phytophagous on almost all groups of plants.

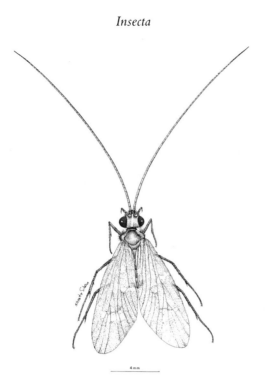

Figure 118. *Phyllocius fenestratus* Flint, Calamoceratidae (Trichoptera).

Lepidoptera is today the second largest order of insects after Coleoptera, although eventually more Hymenoptera will probably be described. Approximately 115,000 species are found in all tropical, temperate, and boreal zones. In South America several families of butterflies exist which are found nowhere else in the world. The family Morphoidae consists of only about 50 species, ranging from central Mexico southward to Uruguay and Paraguay. All species are large and white or metallic blue in color. They are commonly encountered in Amazonian forests where they make a striking impression. They are so distinctive, in fact, that a religious sect has temporarily arisen, distinguished from other sects by their metallic blue robes.

Two other exclusively Neotropical groups of butterflies are the Heliconiidae and Ithomiidae. These two families often have elaborate markings on the wings which vary from area to area. Several early naturalists were surprised to find that color patterns of one species were frequently also found in other butterflies only distantly related. Henry W. Bates and Franz Müller developed theories of mimicry based on similarities of color patterns. Keith Brown Jr. (1979) has used the variation in color pattern over extensive areas to develop a theory of Neotropical biological refugia during the last ice ages, when tropical areas were drier than now.

The Amazon Basin is also the home of *Thysania agrippina* Kramer, a noctuid moth with a wing expanse of up to 30 cm, making it the largest moth in the world. These moths are quite common in central Amazonia, where they appear similar to large white bats fluttering around lights at night.

In Reserva Ducke, Lepidoptera were found in all types of traps, but were most conspicuous in 15 m light traps and the flight trap. In the 15 m light traps they were the second most commonly encountered order, after Diptera (table 4). More importantly, Lepidoptera made up more than 52% of the arthropod biomass in these same traps (table 9). In the flight trap,

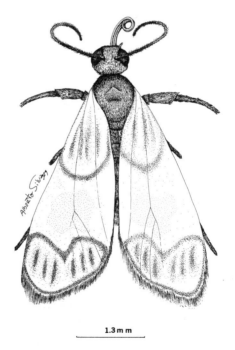

1.3 m m

Figure 119.   Pyralidae (Lepidoptera).

Lepidoptera was the third most common order after Diptera and Hymenoptera (table 6). Further, in the flight trap Lepidoptera made up more than 8% of the dry weight biomass. Thus, the data indicate a very important role for Lepidoptera in the tropical forest ecosystem, especially in the forest canopy where much of the primary production is taking place.

ORDER: DIPTERA

Diptera, or true flies, encompasses groups as diverse as mosquitoes, horseflies, and gall midges. They all have in common a holometabolous development and modification of the hindwings into tiny halteres. Larvae may be aquatic (Culicidae) to saprophagous (Calliphoridae and Phoridae) to leaf miners (Agromyzidae) to predators (many Syrphidae), to external parasites (Hippoboscidae), to internal parasites (Mydaidae and Oestridae). Adults have just as varied a habitus, from flowers to feces to man.

Diptera is the fourth largest order of insects with about 90,000 described species. Flies are everywhere, not only abundant in species, but abundant in number of individuals. This is very apparent in Reserva Ducke as elsewhere. Diptera were found in all traps and were the dominant arthropod group in all counts. This dominance varied from 34% in the baited pitfall traps to 91% in 15 m light traps. In terms of arthropod biomass, dipterans are generally less dominant, because of their small size. Dipteran contribution to the biomass ranged from 49% in the flight trap (mostly horse flies) to about 2% in the baited pitfall traps. Thus, after beetles, Diptera may make the most significant contribution to arthropod biomass in Neotropical forest ecosystems, despite their small size.

Family: Culicidae

Culicidae, or mosquitoes, are a familiar group of small to medium-sized insects with characteristic wing venation, long proboscis, and many-segmented antennae which are plumose in males. Larvae are aquatic in lentic or lotic situations and feed on microorganisms in the water. A few, like *Psorophora* and *Toxorhynchites*, have predaceous larvae. Mosquitoes are impor-

tant vectors in the Amazon Basin of malaria, yellow fever and
arboviruses.

Culicidae is a fairly large family with 2960 described species
(Knight & Stone 1977). Of these, 411 are known from Brazil.
Within Reserva Ducke, mosquitoes are abundant, but taken
successfully only in certain types of traps; in this study primarily
in the light traps. Culicidae accounted for more than 10% of
the arthropod biomass in the 1 m light traps, while accounting
for less than 1% in the 15 m traps and almost nothing in the
other traps.

Family: Micropezidae

Micropezidae, or stilt-legged flies, are medium-sized, elongate
insects with long legs, usually banded (fig. 120). Some species
mimic ants quite closely, folding the wings over the body.
Larvae live in feces and rotting fruit while adults congregate
in moist, forested situations and bathrooms.

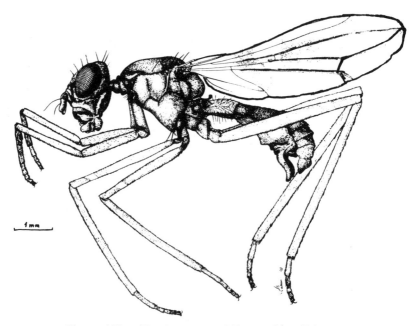

Figure 120.   *Taenioptera* sp., Micropezidae (Diptera).

Micropezidae is a medium-sized family which is primarily tropical. Eighty-five species are known from Brazil (Steyskal, 1968a). In Reserva Ducke, micropezids were found in emergence traps (17) and 1 m light traps (5), but never in 15 m light traps. However, by far the most effective trapping techniques were the flight trap (825) and baited pitfall traps (785). The flight trap data (graph 88) indicates a June population peak, while the baited pitfall traps also indicate a strong emergence peak in June with a secondary peak in January (graph 89). As noted in graph 90, this fluctuation in populations is found in traps baited with feces ($P < .001$). Traps baited with fish show low catches throughout the year. There was a significant difference in attractancy using different killing-preservative fluids ($P < .001$), with picric acid more attractive.

Family: Neriidae

Neriidae, or cactus flies, is a family of small to medium-sized flies with long legs and porrect antennae with the arista situated at the end of the third segment (fig. 121). Little is known about larval biology, but the two species known from North America

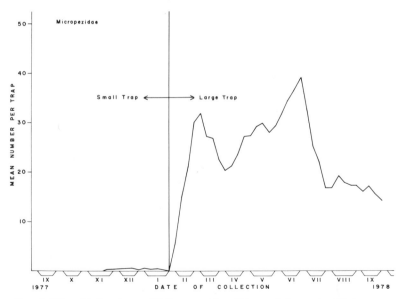

Graph 88. Collections of Micropezidae (Diptera) from the flight trap.

Graph 89.   Collections of Micropezidae (Diptera) from baited pitfall traps.

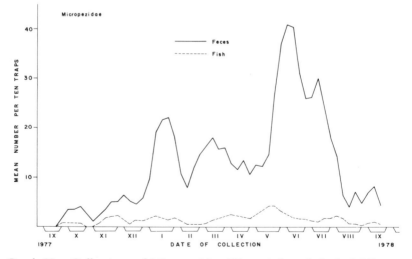

Graph 90.   Collections of Micropezidae (Diptera) from baited pitfall traps, segregated by baits.

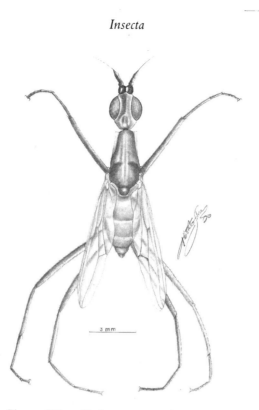

Figure 121. *Nerius* sp., Neriidae (Diptera).

live in decaying cactus, and hence the name cactus flies. This is probably a misnomer, because obviously species from central amazonian forests are not living in cactus.

Neriidae is a small family almost completely restricted to tropical areas. Steyskal (1968b) lists 11 genera and 39 species from South and Central America. Of these only 3 genera and 15 species are known from Brazil. In Reserva Ducke, nine neriids were found in the flight trap. They were collected occasionally, throughout the year.

Family: Psychodidae (subfamily Phlebotominae)

Psychodidae, or moth flies, are small, moth-like flies with hairy wings and bodies (fig. 122). Adults are often encountered in and around sewage drains or other moist places. Larvae live in decaying vegetable matter.

Within the family Psychodidae is the subfamily Phlebotominae, or sand flies, which are minute, long-legged flies. Adult
females feed on blood, and are carriers of several diseases, most
prominently leishmaniasis in the Amazon Basin.

Phlebotominae is a rather large subfamily, with 300 described
species from the New World, and Martins et al. (1978) theorizes
that the number may eventually reach 400 species, or more.
There are now three recognized genera of New World sand flies
(*Brumptomyia* França & Parrot, *Lutzomyia* França, and *Warileya*
Hertig) with *Lutzomyia* containing the vast majority of species.
Within Reserva Ducke, sand flies were collected from all types
of traps, except baited pitfall traps.

Over 20,000 sand flies were collected over the study period
of which over 80% were caught in the 15 m light traps (graph

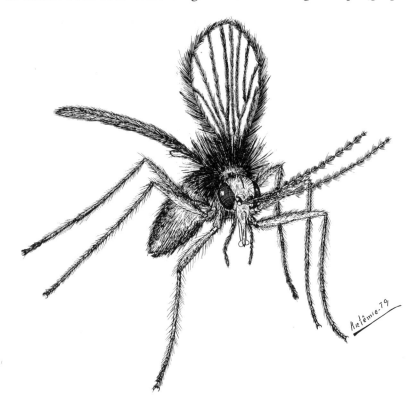

Figure 122.   *Lutzomyia umbratilis* Ward & Freiha, Phlebotominae (Diptera).

91). The 1 m light traps and flight traps equally caught the remainder with a very small quantity coming in the emergence traps. The predominant species captured were *Lutzomyia umbratilis* and *Lutzomyia anduzei*, the principal and secondary vector of cutaneous leishmaniasis in the area. The high number of sand flies caught was due to the design of the C.D.C. light traps baited with CO_2. Only three *Brumptomyia pintoi* were caught, all other 49 species being in the genus *Lutzomyia*. The light trap data (graph 91) indicates a population peak both at 15 and 1 m. "Bonanza" populations (great numbers in one trap due to ideal conditions) occurred in late May in one of the 15 m traps. This occurred when a double compliment of traps had been set out, yet it occurred in one of the traps which was there for the entire study period. Because of the small size of these insects (± 2 mm) the biomass was insignificant.

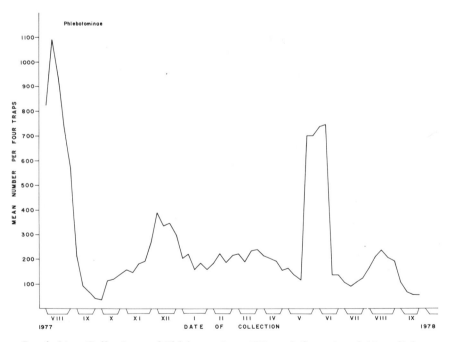

Graph 91.   Collections of Phlebotominae (Diptera) from 1 and 15 m light traps.

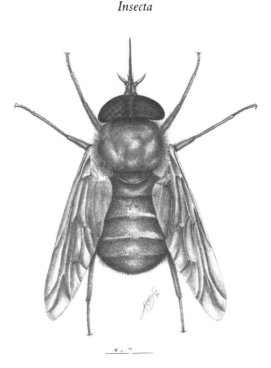

Figure 123. Tabanidae (Diptera).

Family: Tabanidae

Tabanidae, or horseflies and deerflies, are medium- to large-sized, robust flies (fig. 123) with large eyes (contiguous in males). The females are blood-feeders with piercing mouthparts and are often a serious nuisance, buzzing around the body of man or other animals, until finally landing and commencing to feed. Often the bite is accompanied by sharp pain, which can cause serious diminuation of weight or milk production among livestock. Adult females are known carriers of human diseases in some parts of the world. Larvae are aquatic predators of other soft-bodied insects.

Tabanidae is a large family of around 3000 described species. In South and Central America 995 species are recorded in 47 genera. In Reserva Ducke, tabanids were collected only in the flight trap, but within this trap constituted almost 38% of all arthropod biomass in early October (table 10). Flight trap data indicate a September–October emergence peak of tabanids (graph 92).

ORDER: HYMENOPTERA

Hymenoptera, or bees, wasps, ants, and their allies, are a diverse assemblage of four-winged, holometabolous insects, which have several times developed social behavior and forms of communication. In some families the modified ovipositor has become a stinging mechanism. Larvae are generally of two types: among the primitive Symphyta, larvae are similar to lepidopterous caterpillars, while among the Apocrita the legless larva appears similar to scarab beetle larvae.

Hymenoptera is, today, the third largest order of insects, but because of the large number of small and parasitic forms yet

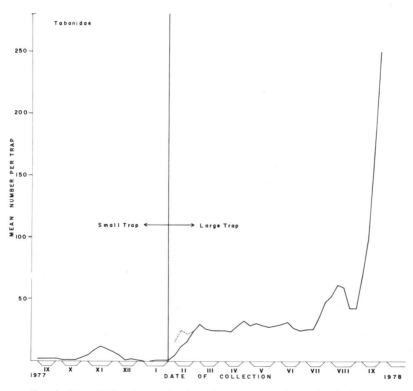

Graph 92.   Collections of Tabanidae (Diptera) from the flight trap.

undescribed, the Hymenoptera will probably surpass the Lepidoptera. Approximately 108,000 species have already been described (Borror et al. 1976) worldwide. These include *Pepsis*, a pompilid wasp with a 70 mm body length, down to some myrmarid egg parasites with a size of 0.2 mm. In Reserva Ducke the hymenopterans caught in the traps sometimes fluctuated greatly, reflecting their social behavior. For example, occasionally army ants would burrow under an emergence trap, and large numbers of ants would then be caught that week. Occasionally large numbers of bees would come to a baited pitfall trap, then there would be none for several weeks. Hymenoptera was the second most common order of arthropods in 1 m light traps, emergence traps and the flight trap. In terms of biomass contribution, Hymenoptera accounted for 11% of all arthropods in 15 m light traps, 17% in the flight trap, 11% in emergence traps and 7% in traps baited with fish. Thus, Hymenoptera plays a large and significant role in energy turnover in the tropical forest ecosystem.

Family: Apidae

Apidae, or bees, are medium-sized to large insects with robust, hairy bodies and bifurcate hairs. They are similar to Anthophoridae, but with vestigal maxillary palpi, broad genae and corbiculae on the hindlegs. Most species are social with larvae reared in cells with food provisioned by adults. Adults feed on nectar and pollen.

The bees found in Reserva Ducke pertain to the tribe Euglossini of Bombinae and the tribe Meliponini of the Apinae. Euglossini, or orchid bees, are found only in tropical America and are usually associated with orchid pollination. They were occasionally caught in the flight trap. Meliponini, or stingless bees, reach their greatest development in South America. These bees were encountered in the baited pitfall traps, generally in large numbers on infrequent occasions. It is not known what lured them into the traps on these occasions. In terms of biomass, average numbers were too small to amount to more than 0.95% of hymenopteran biomass.

Family: Dryinidae

Dryinidae, or dryinid wasps, are small to medium-sized parasitic wasps, characterized by the pincer-like fore tarsi and occasional winglessness of females (fig. 124). Larvae are internal and external parasites of Homoptera, and polyembryony can occur among species of this family. The pincer-like fore tarsi are used to hold hosts for oviposition.

Richards (1953) recognized 54 genera of Dryinidae. These insects are not common in the Manaus area. In Reserva Ducke dryinids were encountered only in the flight trap on five occasions: 30 May, 29 Aug., 6 Sept., 20 Sept., and 27 Sept. Although the number of individuals was quite low, a September emergence is indicated.

Family: Eucharitidae

Eucharitidae, or eucharitid wasps, are small, black, humpbacked insects with long thoracic spines (fig. 125). As members of the Chalcoidea, they have very reduced wing venation. Lar-

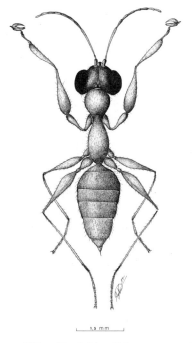

Figure 124.   Dryinidae (Hymenoptera).

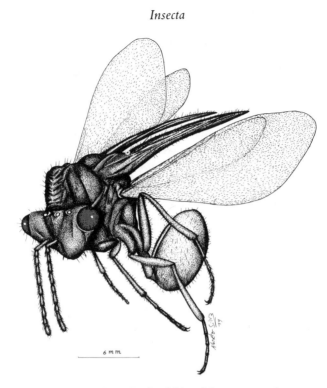

Figure 125.   Eucharitidae (Hymenoptera).

vae are parasitic on ant pupae. Eggs are laid randomly and in
large numbers on vegetation. When the first instar larva hatches,
it seeks out an adult worker, and is carried to the nest. Once
inside the nest, it seeks out and feeds upon an ant pupa.

Eucharitidae are not frequently encountered. In Reserva
Ducke they were recorded from 15 m light traps (1) and emergence traps (28). They seem to be most often collected during
the dry season from May to September (graph 93).

Family: Formicidae

Formicidae, or ants, are small to large insects with elbowed
antennae and first abdominal segment bearing a node, which
is strongly separated from the rest of the abdomen. All ants
form colonies of from 15 to several thousand individuals. A
winged queen will start a new colony after a nuptial flight. Her
wings are shed, and she will produce a first brood of workers,
who then take over maintenance of the colony. Subsequently,

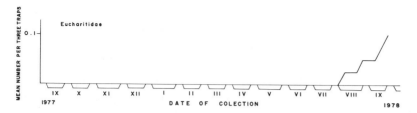

Graph 93.   Collections of Eucharitidae (Hymenoptera) from the emergence
traps.

other workers, males, and queens are produced. The colony
may exist in the soil, in trees, inside plant galls, etc. Workers
care for eggs and larvae, feeding and protecting them when
necessary. Food habits vary greatly within this family. Army
ants are predaceous and saprophagous, feeding on dead or living
animal flesh. Some species of *Atta* are leaf-cutting ants which
carry the leaf fragments back to the nest to create below-ground
fungus gardens. Leaf-cutting ants can be serious pests in some
areas, cutting virtually all green vegetation within a wide radius
of the nest. Schade (1973) has found that leaf-cutting ant nests
may have entrances up to 500 m from the center of the nest.
Other ants are nectar feeders, cutting small holes in the bases
of flowers to obtain nectar. Some plants have even developed
extra-floral nectaries in exchange for the protection given the
plant by ants (Janzen 1966).

Kempf (1972) records 7 subfamilies, 34 tribes, 147 genera,
and 2233 species from the Neotropical Region. The Neotropical
Region shows the highest degree of generic endemism of all
regions with 65 genera (Brown 1973). In Reserva Ducke, ants
were at times abundant, at other times much less so, indicating
their colonial nature. In terms of biomass, ants accounted for
5% of arthropods in the 15 m light trap; almost 3% in the flight
trap; almost 8% in emergence traps; and less than 1 to 7% in
baited pitfall traps. Ants were more abundant in traps baited
with fish then feces.

Family: Megachilidae

Megachilidae, or leaf-cutting bees, are medium-sized to large
bees with a relatively large head, and two submarginal wing

cells of about equal length. Adults line the nest cavity with neatly cut leaf fragments. Nests are usually placed in a natural cavity, usually wood.

Megachilidae is a fairly common family, and in western North America is an important pollinator of alfalfa. In Reserva Ducke few individuals were encountered, but those collected were notable for their size and coloration. A few were metallic blue or green, somewhat resembling the Euglossine bees of Apidae. In terms of biomass, these large bees accounted for about 1.5% of arthropod biomass in the flight trap.

GENERAL CONSIDERATIONS

UNUSUAL AND INTERESTING COLLECTIONS

The tropical American forest appears to have little animal life at first glance, but upon closer inspection is teeming with life in the forest canopy, in tree trunks, in the soil. To an insect taxonomist more accustomed to north and south temperate insect faunas, the Amazon Basin contains many pleasant surprises. We have added this chapter to give the reader a better understanding of some of the taxonomic "pitfalls" and esthetic pleasures of this forest habitat.

In studying the bristle-tail orders Archaeognatha and Thysanura, most students of North American entomology are only familiar with two families, Machilidae and Lepismatidae. Borror et al. (1976) only lists four families, the other two being quite rare. Machilidae and Lepismatidae exist in the Amazon Basin, and as elsewhere are seen scurrying about in dark corners of buildings. But, an entomologist working in the field of Amazonia encounters a very different fauna: Meinertellidae, Ateluridae and Nicoletiidae (figs. 20, 21), the first of which is quite common.

The only ephemeropteran collected during our study in Reserva Ducke was a most unusual specimen. In addition to the two normal compound eyes that almost all insects possess, this individual appeared to have two additional compound eyes extending dorsally from the top of the head (fig. 22). Edmonds et al. (1976) mentions two families of may-flies which possess these "turbinate" eyes. Our specimen keys out to the baetid genus *Baetodes*, although as Edmonds states "generic limits in the family are generally vague and poorly defined."

Upon studying the soil arthropod fauna, one of the first insects to be encountered is a tiny, rounded insect with heavily sclerotized wings that are unmistakable beetle elytra (fig. 33). The only problem with immediately calling it a beetle is that the insect also has sucking mouthparts, like a hemipteran. They are common on the forest floor and the highly reduced hind-wings indicate that this insect cannot fly. It does closely resemble the somewhat larger hemipteran family called Pleidae, except that the antennae are four-segmented and long, quite unlike the short, cryptic antennae of Pleidae. The antennae are, in fact, the key to proper identification of this family, as the first two segments are short and stout while the last two are long and thin, indicating the hemipteran superfamily Dipsocoroidea, and a close look at the position of the eyes reveals it to be Schizopteridae. McAtee and Malloch (1925), in their monographic revision of this group mention four genera having heavily sclerotized forewings: *Hoplonannus brunnea* McAtee and Malloch from Guatemala, *Ptenidiophyes mirabilis* Reuter from southern Brazil, *Glyptocombus saltator* Heidemann from U.S.A. and *Hypselosome boops* McAtee and Malloch from China. Wygodzinsky (1948) mentioned that in some genera females are brachypterous, or sclerotized, although in a few species both sexes are beetle-like. Wygodzinsky (personal communication) mentions these insects as being common inhabitants of the tropical forest. Emsley (1969) has revised the family Schizopteridae, which now contains 33 genera and 142 species. All sclerotized individuals encountered at Reserva Ducke were females.

Because of its productivity, the flight trap continued to be utilized after the official end of the study. One week after the study ended (3 Oct. 1978) a very large and strange homopteran was taken from the flight trap. It was 35 mm long and had an extremely long protuberance in front of its head (fig. 31). It was easily noted as being in the Fulgoroidea. Within this superfamily, the family Fulgoridae, or lantern-flies, are well-known for their size and precephalic protuberances. However, this individual did not have the reticulate wing venation of Fulgoridae. Instead, it showed all the key characters of Dictyopharidae, which also is known for its precephalic protuberances, but generally is of much smaller size. Dr. Lois O'Brien of Florida State University, Tallahassee, Florida, was kind enough to confirm that this insect was indeed a dictyopharid. In fact, it was *Lappida longirostris* Schmidt, previously known only from Panama (Metcalf 1946).

Almost all adult insects have four wings, or in some cases,

such as parasitic insects, the wings have been secondarily lost. The major exception to this statement are the true flies, where hindwings have been reduced to tiny gyroscopic organs. Some beetles and Strepsiptera have forewings reduced to small, sclerotized pads, but some remnant of the forewings remains. Additionally, a few groups of Ephemeroptera have completely lost their forewings; but on 8 Aug. 1978, a totally different, two-winged insect appeared in the flight trap. It was only about 4 mm long; with elongate, tubular mouthparts; long antennae, and what appeared to be hindwings held rigidly out to the sides of the body, airplane fashion. The mouthparts suggested a homopteran, and indeed, this insect turned out to be a male scale insect of the family Monophlebiidae. Insects with only hindwings are quite unusual, and homopterans with long, hairy antennae are also unusual. However, in tropical areas of America and Asia these insects are encountered much more frequently.

The insectan order Neuroptera has been little studied in the Amazon Basin. The larger and more conspicuous representatives have been described over the years in various publications by a multitude of authors, but little is known of the smaller representatives, and nothing at all has been done on biology. Thus, it was not too surprising that we encountered Coniopterygidae and Dilaridae for the first time in the Amazon Basin. The Dilaridae are of interest because of the pectinate antennae in males (fig. 37) and ovipositors of females. Hemerobiidae are unusual because of their scarcity. This family is quite common both north and south of the Amazon Basin, but is extremely difficult to find in the Amazon Basin. Our records are the first in Amazonia in this century, and only the second ever. One additional family may yet be found within the Andean uplift of Amazonia. The family Osmylidae is found in southern Brazil and the Andean Region as far north as Ecuador, but has not yet been found in Amazonia.

A cephalic horn is not a common structure among insects, it being most frequently found in the scarab subfamily Dynastinae. However, during the study we encountered members of the Tenebrionidae and Cisidae with cephalic horns, and some Nitidulidae with dorsally projecting mandibles. The reason for this structural convergence is not known.

One additional species of beetle has not yet been identified to family, although several very knowledgeable beetle specialists have seen our specimens. They are about 5 mm long, fuscous in color, with 5-5-4 tarsal segmentation. The hindlegs are exceptionally large and the elytra are short, exposing the last two abdominal segments. The names Meloidae and Eucnetidae have been suggested, but neither seems to fit this species of insect well.

On 21 Feb. a fly with extremely long, stalked eyes was found in a 15 m light trap (fig. 126). In equatorial forests of Africa and Asia flies with stalked eyes in the family Diopsidae are frequently encountered, but this family does not exist in South America, and the position of the antennae were quite different in the insect we collected. A quick glance at figure 34.28c in *The Insects of Australia* revealed a strong similarity between our insect and *Achias australis* in the Platystomatidae. Later, Dr. Wayne Matthis of the U.S. National Museum was gracious enough to identify this insect for us as *Plaglocephalus latifrons* Hendel. This species is in the family Otitidae and is known from Bolivia to Panama (Steyskal 1968c), but this is the first record we know of from Brazil.

Figure 126.   *Plaglocephalus latifrons* (Hendes), Otitidae (Diptera).

The families Otitidae and Platystomatidae are recognized by Diptera specialists as being closely related, but that two genera should develop such similar stalked eyes independently seems very dubious. It seems logical that a reevaluation of the evolution of these two "families" is called for.

One day, among the other material being sorted from the traps appeared an insect which at first was hard to identify to order. At a quick glance it looked like an ant, with normal ant size, coloration, and body shape; and it was wingless. Upon closer inspection it could be noticed that it had what appeared to be raptorial forelegs—a tiny mantid mimicking an ant. But, the raptorial forelegs were not right, only the tarsal segments formed the grasping section of the leg. Finally, it was decided that this insect must be a hymenopteran. It was the family Dryinidae, which is seldom encountered in North America, but is a fairly common family of homopteran parasites in tropical areas.

These experiences, and many others, have given us a much better appreciation of the diversity of form and structure encountered in American tropical areas.

BIOMASS

The biomass of an ecological area is an extremely difficult entity to quantify, especially when the biomass selected is hard to observe and always in motion. The traps at Reserva Ducke allowed us a clear look at some of the arthropod activity in a tropical forest, but the results can only be extrapolated from the data base, in this case five types of traps. We know that each type of trap is somewhat biased in favor of certain types of arthropods, with certain modes of living and certain modes of behavior. For example, a flight trap will catch very few scarab beetles despite their frequency in the forest, simply because scarab beetles drop rather than rise when encountering the side of the trap. However, taken together, these traps can present a dim picture of what is actually happening within the forest. Tables 3 to 7 give a numerical presentation of those arthropods coming into the traps on four selected dates throughout the year. However, this information tells us little about the arthropod biomass in the same traps. Because taking the dry weight of an insect destroys the insect for further study, we waited until the last week of the study to measure arthropod biomass. Tables 8 to 15 give the results of the biomass study on 4 Oct. 1978. Statistically, the insect collections for this week do not appear significantly different from that of the previous three weeks samples.

One problem immediately apparent is that only the emergence traps record biomass from a known area. All other traps draw in moving arthropods from an unknown distance. However, we do know that the beetle family Dascillidae was emerging from the emergence traps at a rate of 13 from 27 m² over a four week period. This comes to 4815 beetles emerging per hectare. The flight trap caught 123 dascillids, or the total emergence from 59 m² of forest floor.

During the 56-week course of the study, 3470 Staphylinidae emerged from the 27 emergence traps set up on consecutive months. This amounts to 3.36 beetles per m² per week. During the last 34 weeks of the study 826 staphylinids were collected in the flight trap, perhaps signifying an effective trapping area of only 7.2 m². This smaller flight trapping area for staphylinids than for dascillids could reflect the greater aerial movement of the latter family.

However, this result could also indicate a difference in effectiveness of emergence traps as a trapping technique. Dascillids have been shown to emerge for only a very short period of time during the year in the study site. We also know that larvae live in the soil surface litter. Thus, emergence traps are an effective means of indicating the emerging population of this one brood per year. But, Staphylinidae is present in the soil litter at all times, probably producing more than one generation per year. In this case, the emergence trap reduces the likelihood of staphylinids using this particular square meter of soil subsequently. Thus, the number of staphylinid beetles taken from the emergence traps diminishes with time (graph 83), and is no longer a good indicator of population abundance.

Despite these differences in behavior, certain trends are clear. Orthopterans are very large contributors to the arthropod biomass at ground level, while Lepidoptera and Diptera appear to be very important herbivores in the forest canopy. Among herivorous beetles, Cerambycidae, Chrysomelidae, Elateridae, Curculionidae, and Scolytidae are most important. Fungus feeding families, such as Ptiliidae, Leptodiridae, Erotylidae, and others are present in large numbers, but their average size is small, and consequent biomass contribution minor. As mentioned in Penny et al. (1978), many ground dwelling beetles appear to be mite predators, such as Staphylinidae, Pselaphidae, Scydmaenidae, and Carabidae. Approximately a quarter of the arthropod biomass in the emergence traps appeared to be social insects (Isoptera and Formicidae), and to a lesser extent were present in other traps as well. The development of socialism among insects may have been one effective way of coping with hard-to-get-at nutrient resources in the tropical forest environment.

Protein sources, in the form of feces, carrion, or blood appears to attract large numbers of insects in the tropical forest. Over a third of all biomass in the flight trap was tabanids. Over 10% of the biomass in 1 m light traps was Culicidae. A comparison of emergence trap and baited pitfall trap records indicates that scarab beetles were being attracted to feces and carrion from a minimum sized area of 4337.5 m^2, or almost ½ hectare.

ECOENERGETICS

Fittkau and Klinge (1973) studied the primary production of a terra firme forest only 38 km from Reserva Ducke. They found a total production of above ground leaves, twigs, stems, plant parasites, fruits and tree trunks to be 730.7 metric tons (mt) per hectare. An additional 225 mt per hectare is produced by below ground root systems, for a total live production of 955.7 mt per hectare.

An additional factor in primary production is the accumulated dead plant tissue which has not been yet recycled. At the study site of Fittkau and Klinge this amounted to 44 mt per hectare of dead wood and 15 mt of fine forest detritus. Thus, the total primary productivity of a central Amazonian forest at any one point in time can be taken to be about 1100 mt per hectare.

The 59 mt per hectare of organic material at the soil surface represents a balance between rate of litter fall and decomposition. Fittkau and Klinge found that the rate of litter fall at their study site was about 11 mt per hectare per year. This would indicate an average rate of decomposition also of 11 mt per hectare per year, or about 5 years for a complete decomposition of material at the soil surface at any one moment.

But, this rate of decomposition is not uniform—leaves, fruit, twigs, and branches decompose at a much faster rate than tree trunks. Klinge and Rodrigues (1968) working again near Manaus found that of this litter fall, 5.6 mt per hectare per year is leaves, or slightly over 50% of all litter fall. Klinge (1972) found that these leaves decompose at a rate of 0.56% per day, while Stark and Holley (1975) found that leaves in Amazonian terra firme forests almost completely decompose in three months, or a rate of 1.11% per day. This is about twice the velocity of Klinge's findings. In either case, all leaves are decomposed in six months or less.

Estimates of the fruit portion of litter fall were about 2.0 mt per hectare (Fittkau and Klinge 1973). Klinge (1972) reports the rate of decomposition of fruits to be 2.3 per cent per day, or total decomposition within 1.5 months.

The remaining portion, the woody litter, makes up 4.35 mt per hectare per year, or 39.5% of all litter fall. Using the litter fall for the leaf and fruit portions and their rates of decomposition, it is quickly apparent that it is the woody portion which has the slowest rate of decomposition and greatest litter accumulation. Fittkau and Klinge (1973) found about 75% of the litter present at any one moment to be woody tissue, even though only 39% of litter falling is woody. Thus, the rate of decomposition is 0.027% per day, or a complete decomposition of all woody material in 10.11 years.

Of the 59 mt of dead plant tissue per hectare, the energy and nutrients can leave this trophic level in one of three ways: a) the nutrients and organic matter can be leached out of the soil and into the fluvial system; b) insects and other invertebrates can attack it directly, causing decomposition; or c) direct recycling by mycorrhizal fungus can put these nutrients directly back into primary production.

Went and Stark (1968) have shown that in a tropical forest most plant roots are close to the soil surface, oftentimes even forming a mat upon the surface. In close association with these roots are many mycelia of mycorrhizal fungi which are also intertwined with the decaying plant material. Whenever mycelia of mycorrhiza are present the decaying material is soft and fluid. Often the associated roots do not even have root hairs, and the absence of the mycorrhiza severely restricts subsequent plant growth (Briscoe 1960). It seems clear that the mycorrhiza act as decomposer and transport agent for recycling plant nutrients. Janzen (1976) has suggested a further evolutionary plant modification to enhance direct recycling of nutrients. He notes that many tropical trees are hollow and that this hollow center is often filled with fallen plant tissue. Thus, through decomposition (perhaps by microrrhiza ?) the nutrients are already placed most effectively for plant uptake.

How much of the 59 mt of dead plant material per hectare is directly recycled to the living plants? Stark and Holley (1975) found that almost none of the leaf litter was directly leaving the forest ecosystem in the form of physically or chemically "washed out" nutrients. Further, little bacterial activity was noted on terrestrial sites. Almost all decomposition activity was carried out by fungi and insect activity. However, it was impossible to tell precisely what percentage could be attributed to insects, what to fungus. It was noted that nutrient content of the leaves did not decrease with time, indicating that fungus and insects consumed whole areas, not selectively taking areas of high nutrient content for one or several chemicals.

Singer and Araujo (1979) have listed major species of fungi involved in litter decomposition in central Amazonia, but no biomass figures are given.

Our studies with emergence traps demonstrate that within the forest litter layer .019 mt/hectare/year of arthropod biomass are emerging from the soil or crawling over the surface. Of this arthropod biomass, approximately .0103 mt per hectare can be considered litter feeders, .0007 mt per hectare are mycetophagous, .0026 mt per hectare are root feeders, and the remaining .0053 mt per hectare are predators and parasites (table 17). These figures are only approximate because in the order Diptera, for example, there are litter feeders, mycetophagous flies, and perhaps others. It was necessary to decide which was the predominant category. However, it can be seen that very little (.019 mt) of the 59 mt of litter falling to the forest floor is directly consumed by insects. The vast majority of nutrients are probably quickly recycled into the plants, both directly and indirectly, but as yet no figures are available to prove this point. It also is not known what type of fungus the mycetophagous insects are feeding on. Thus, the role of these insects could conceivably be to help recycle nutrients by feeding on the fungus-feeding fungi, or the role could be detrimental, feeding on fungi which themselves recycle nutrients.

Not all the 59 mt of material falling to the forest floor is wood and leaves. Fruit falls are popular gathering places for both vertebrate and invertebrate herbivores in the tropical forest. This contribution to the biomass is often concentrated, and thus difficult to assess accurately. Additionally, almost nothing is known about the average biomass of the frugivorous herbivores because of the distances from which they are often attracted. Thus, the contribution to the biomass of fallen fruit and its herbivores remain unknown, and consequently the contribution to the flow of energy from detritus to fungus is also unknown.

The part of the biomass actively consumed by herbivores is the most difficult to assess and the part where most work needs to be done. A measure of herbivory cannot be taken directly by subtracting leaf fall biomass from primary production, simply because we do not know for how long a leaf remains on the tree before falling in this evergreen forest. And, of course, lacking data on these herbivores limits discussion of further energy and nutrient dispersal in the food chain.

As can be seen, what we still do not know far surpasses what we do know, and every step of advancement only fragments and further complicates further progress. However, by patiently pursuing each step, the future may yet reveal many more secrets of life within the tropical forest, a life dominated by its insect life.

COMPARISONS AND CONCLUSIONS

Richness:

The wet, lowland tropical forests have long been considered to be extremely rich in plant and vertebrate animal diversity. Brown (1973) has written of the ant fauna, "it is clear that the tropical forests have at least the greatest *diversity* at both genus and species levels." Brown also found twice as many endemic ant genera in the Neotropical Region as any other region.

Our study also indicates that the richness of land forms, plant life and vertebrate animal life found in the Amazon Basin is complemented by the insect richness. As can be seen from even so limited a study as this one, richness of species and families in the terra firme forest is immense. Even aquatic families such as Sisyridae (Neuroptera), Agrionidae (Odonata), Perlidae (Plecoptera) and many others can occasionally be collected far from any water sources. The warm temperatures and continuously high humidity are very amenable to insects which desiccate easily.

Although few groups from the study have been thoroughly studied yet at the species level, the first results are indicative of high species richness. New (1980) has found that in one superfamily of Psocoptera (Epipsocetae) 31 species were found in the traps, and 27 of them were undescribed species. Altogether, 84 species of Psocoptera were collected. Ubirajara Martins has found 43 genera and 53 species of Cerambycidae in our samples. Additionally, 50 species of blood-sucking sand flies and 15 genera and 36 species of Neuroptera have been collected in the traps.

However, these figures by themselves have little meaning, except when compared to other areas. Such comparisons reveal to some degree the magnitude of this rickness. The 84 species of Psocoptera from the Reserva Ducke traps compares quite favorably with the 25 species known from Mt. Desert, Maine (Procter 1946) and is more than twice as many species as are known from New York (Leonard 1928) or North Carolina (Wray 1967). The 50 species of blood-sucking sand flies found in the traps represents about 17% of all species known from the Neotropical Region. Neuroptera are insects which reach greatest abundance in dry, sandy areas, with many larvae cofined to living in dry sand. Yet, more than 3% of all species known from the Neotropical Region were taken from traps in this one locality.

Howden and Nealis (1975) have questioned statements by Fittkau and Klinge of low insect numbers in Amazonia. Howden and Nealis based their studies on collections of scarab beetles near Leticia, Colombia. Using pitfall traps, they found 60 species of scarabs in two different habitats. Fifty-six of these species were collected in primary forest. In the pitfall traps at Reserva Ducke 61 species and 19,300 individual scarabs were collected, thus reaffirming the scarab richness documented by Howden and Nealis 1000 km farther west.

Perhaps a comparison of insect richness is best observed in the soil litter fauna, where more data exist. Williams (1941) found 6 genera of termites in samples from Panama, while Bandeira (1979) found 15 genera in a central Amazonian forest. Williams (1941) found one family of Psocoptera in soil samples, while our emergence traps yielded 10 families and 13 species. Willis (1976) found 11 families of beetles in the soil of a forested area of Panama. Dammerman (1938) found five families of beetles in the soil litter of East Java and Krakatoa. Goodnight and Goodnight (1956) found seven families in the soil litter samples from southern Mexico. Our findings of 18 families in litter samples and 64 beetle families emerging into the ground eclectors both emphasize the richness obtainable in central Amazonian soils, and bring into question the value of the much smaller samples from the other areas.

Thus, in terms of both families and species, the Amazonian terra firme forest seems to be very rich.

A note of caution has to be injected with these statistics. From the traps in Reserva Ducke, more species of Achilidae (a little known family of Homoptera) were obtained than have been recorded for all South America. This would seem to indicate an almost unheard of richness at the study site. However, Henk Wolda (1980) has found similar richness among Achilidae in light traps in Panama. In fact, it seems that wherever intensive collections are made in the tropics, many more species are found than are presently recognized. Thus, true richness can only be properly assessed when this group (and others) has been more intensively studied taxonomically.

Number of Individuals and Biomass:

Although we feel that the amount of insect life present (in terms of both biomass and numbers) is much greater than Fittkau and Klinge's impressions, it is still true that great swarms of insects do not occur, contrary to popular belief. Perhaps the Cerambycidae (Coleoptera) can serve as a good example. Although there were 53 species collected, these came from only 194 individuals. We have also noted that for other groups, such as Phlebotominae, Fulgoridae, and Achilidae, the number of individuals per species is quite low. However, the few most common species can be quite common.

Estimates of total numbers of soil insects have now been reported from a number of temperate and tropical forest sites. Strickland (1945) using a flotation method found an estimated 25 thousand arthropods per m^2 in a Trinidad forest. Van der Drift (1963) collected 51 thousand arthropods per m^2 using Berlese funnels in a Surinam forest. Greenslade and Greenslade (1968) extracted an average of 92 thousand individuals per m^2 using Tullgren funnels on a forest site in the Solomon Islands. However, recorded arthropod densities in temperate soils generally are greater than tropical soils, and occasionally far surpasses any estimate yet achieved in tropical soils. Gist and Crossley (1975) estimated 65 thousand arthropods per m^2 in a North Carolina mixed hardwood forest. Salt et al. (1948) reported 248 thousand arthropods per m^2 in a temperate pasture, and estimates of individual groups range as high as 38 to 230 thousand Collembola per m^2 in an English moorland (Hale 1966), 78 thousand Collembola in a Japanese forest soil (Kitazawa 1967), and 133 thousand oribatid mites per m^2 of a French forest soil (Berthet 1963).

A comparison of total numbers of insects in our emergence traps for the four weeks when total counts were taken gives the impression that numbers are comparatively low. Gist and Crossley (1975) found many more mites, Collembola, spiders, etc., and a higher biomass in a North Carolina mixed hardwood forest. It must be kept in mind that in our traps only part of the soil fauna will crawl into the collector during any one given week, and catches diminish with time as the soil fauna is trapped. However, from the foregoing studies in other areas, it seems probable that total numbers of arthropods and total biomass of the soils is lower in Reserva Ducke than in temperate areas. The canopy numbers and biomass is still a relatively unknown quantity. Thus, Fittkau and Klinge may be right in stating the total numbers of insects are lower in a central Amazonian forest than in a temperate forest, but more documentation is still needed for convincing conclusions.

Population Fluctuations:

Unlike temperate ecosystems, the tropical ecosystem is active throughout the year. However, this activity is not uniform and, as can be seen by even a brief glance at graphs of population dynamics in Reserva Ducke, this activity is not uniform from one group to another. As shown in tables 3 to 7, there appears to be somewhat higher populations in December and April, two of the rainiest months. However, general insect populations remain high throughout the year, much more so than Wolda (1978a) has found among homopteran populations in Panama, where the dry and rainy reasons are much more distinct, and insect populations strikingly different at different times of the year.

However, few insect families closely follow the seasonal rainfall trends in central Amazonia. Dascillidae (Coleoptera) for example, were collected during a very short period during the dry season. Populational peaks of Staphylinidae (Coleoptera) as a group follow no rainfall patterns in emergence, although individual species may. Wolda (1978a) has found the same pattern in Panama where certain groups, such as Cicadidae (Homoptera) may reach maximum abundance during the dry season when other groups are in sharp decline. Thus, seasonality of insect abundance in the tropics, as noted by Bigger (1976), Wolda, and others is also demonstrated for central Amazonia, but fluctuations may be somewhat dampened by more uniform rainfall.

Yearly population fluctuations, as Wolda (1978b) demonstrated for Homoptera in Panama, are probably also present in Amazonia, but as the study lasted only 13 months, yearly fluctuations cannot be properly determined.

Group Dominance:

Fittkau and Klinge (1973), citing work done by Beck (1970, 1971) state that "the overwhelming predominance of Acarina and Collembola over all other groups (in the soil fauna) is easily recognized." Our results suggest that Diptera and Hymenoptera are of much more importance in terms of both numbers and biomass. Interestingly, the relative proportions of non-insectan arthropods, primitively wingless (apterygote) insects and winged (pterygote) insects is almost the same in Amazonia as it is in northern Europe (Thiede 1977). However, while true flies are an important factor in the Amazonian forest, they are more important in European spruce forests, and their dominance is partially diminished by the greater number of beetles and hymenopterans in Amazonia.

Light trap catches indicate that Lepidoptera play an important role in the forest canopy, converting primary production into insect biomass, although the exact quantity is still unknown.

Grasshoppers and their allies and leaf-feeding beetles appear to find a similar role in the lower forest strata, although once again the exact figures are not known.

Root-feeding groups primarily involve spittlebugs, some planthoppers (Cixiidae), scarab beetles, and click beetles. The woody portion of litter fall is attacked and broken down by large numbers of Isoptera, Scolytidae, and Cerambycidae. The leafy portion is attacked by mites, ptiliid beetles, and others.

Finally, the herbivorous and mycetophagous arthropods are attacked by spiders, wasps, rove beetles, and vertebrates. A schematic representation of this complex flow of nutrients is shown in figure 127.

Other Amazonian Habitats:

A comparison with work done in other types of Amazonian ecosystems gives a clearer idea as to the potential richness of the whole Amazonian fauna. Irmler (1977) has divided the seasonally inundated forests of Amazonia into five distinct types,

PRIMARY   PRODUCTION   1100 mt / hec.

SECONDARY   PRODUCTION (HERBIVORY)?

TERTIARY   PRODUCTION   (PREDATORS + PARASITES) ?

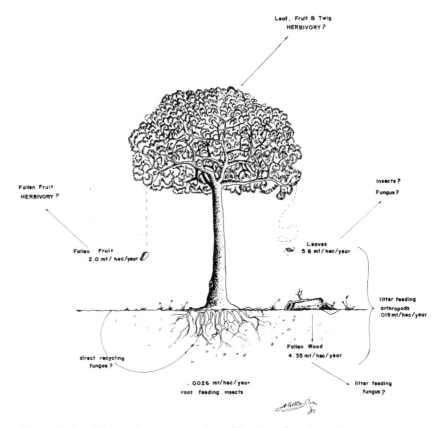

Leaf, Fruit & Twig
HERBIVORY ?

Insects ?
Fungus ?

Fallen Fruit
HERBIVORY ?

Fallen   Fruit
2.0 mt / hec/year

Leaves
5.6 mt/hec/year

litter feeding
arthropods
.019 mt/hec/year

direct recycling
fungus ?

Fallen Wood
4.35 mt/hec/year

litter feeding
fungus ?

.0026 mt/hec/year
root feeding insects

Figure 127.   Schematic representation of nutrient flow in an Amazonian terra
firme forest.

each with its own distinctive insect fauna. Adis (1979a) has
studied one inundation forest near Manaus and found both types
of arthropods and percentage of each major group very different
from the Reserva Ducke terra firme forest samples. For example, more than 3600 symphylans were collected in the in-

undation forest, although only one was collected from Reserva Ducke during our study. Spiders and isopods were also proportionally much more abundant in the inundation forest. Beck (1971) has found that mites found in the inundation forests are the same species as found in the terra firme forests, but the fauna of inundation forests is more impoverished. We have found no evidence to either support or refute the theory of Erwin and Adis (in press) that inundation forests form the driving force for speciation, followed by dispersal into nearby terra firme forests. However, such a theory would predict the results that Beck (1970, 1971) has demonstrated for mite species.

The richness of insects in terra firme forests of Amazonia is, as can be seen from the foregoing discussion, equal or greater than in other temperate and tropical ecosystems. And yet, this is just the beginning of the diversity possible among insects of Amazonia. As Irmler, Adis, Beck, and others have shown, there is a similar, tremendous richness of arthropods in inundated forests. One study cannot hope to do more than elucidate some aspects of this complex mix of ecosystems and encourage further studies in this area. Much remains undiscovered, and the mystery of trying to unravel its biological secrets continues unabated. The river that forsakes the Andes to cross a continent and deposit its waters in the Atlantic Ocean, the river that the people of Amazonia call the River-Sea, still provides the focus for generations of biologists, naturalists, and people simply interested in observing Nature. And, the insects of the Amazon forest are a large part of this mystery and fascination of discovery.

APPENDIX TABLES

Table 1. Chemical Data of a Soil Profile at km. 24 along Manaus–Itacoatiara Highway

CHEMICAL DATA

Profile: 7   Municipality: Manaus

Classification: heavy textured, yellow latosol   Local: km. 24 at 20 m. from Manaus–Itacoatiara Highway

gm/100 gm. of T.F.S.A.

Horizon	Ph	Ca^{+2}	Mg^{+2}	K^+	Na^+	Mn^{+2}	H^+	Al^{+3}	T	S	C	N	MO	SiO_2	Fe_2O_3	Al_{23}	C/N	Ki	Kr	V %	P_2O_5 mg/1000 gm	Ph KCl
A_1	4.6	1.15	0.23	0.11	0.17	0.02	6.07	1.63	8.36	0.66	1.51	1.14	2.60	17.00	1.60	13.77	10.5	2.10	1.95	8	0.61	3.8
A_3	4.4	0.15	0.20	0.07	0.15	0.02	3.25	0.87	4.69	0.57	0.68	0.07	1.14	28.80	2.19	21.16	9.5	2.07	1.94	12	0.55	4.3
B_{21}	4.8	0.15	0.18	0.05	0.10	0.02	2.53	0.27	3.18	0.38	0.50	0.04	0.86	27.20	2.19	23.20	11.2	2.00	1.88	12	trace	4.4
B_{22}	4.8	0.15	0.10	0.08	0.18	0.02	2.39	0.65	3.55	0.51	0.42	0.03	0.72	27.20	2.00	22.95	11.1	2.01	1.91	14	trace	4.4
B_3	5.3	0.15	0.05	0.06	0.12	0.02	1.72	0.43	2.53	0.38	0.26	0.02	0.46	30.20	2.39	24.48	10.7	2.09	1.97	15	trace	4.6

SOURCE: Modified from Falesi et al. (1969).

Table 2. Orders of Arthropoda Collected During Reserva Ducke Study With Method of Collection

Group	Light Trap 1 m.	Light Trap 15 m.	Emergence Trap	Flight Trap	Baited Pitfall Traps
Onychophora			X		
Arachnida	X	X	X	X	X
Scorpionida			X		X
Phalangida			X		
Acari	X		X	X	X
Thelyphonida			X		X
Araneida	X	X	X	X	X
Isopoda			X		X
Diplopoda			X		X
Chilopoda			X		X
Symphyla			X		
Insecta	X	X	X	X	X
Collembola	X		X	X	X
Diplura			X		X
Microcoryphia			X	X	X
Thysanura			X		
Ephemeroptera				X	
Odonata				X	
Orthoptera	X	X	X	X	X
Dermaptera			X	X	X
Isoptera	X	X	X	X	X
Embioptera	X	X	X	X	
Plecoptera				X	
Psocoptera	X	X	X	X	X
Thysanoptera			X	X	X
Hemiptera	X	X	X	X	X
Neuroptera	X	X	X	X	X
Coleoptera	X	X	X	X	X
Strepsiptera	X	X			
Mecoptera	X			X	
Trichoptera				X	
Lepidoptera	X	X	X	X	X
Diptera	X	X	X	X	X
Hymenoptera	X	X	X	X	X

Table 3. Total Count Light Trap: 1 Meter

Group	13 Dec. 77		25 Mar. 78		12 Sept. 78		3 Oct. 78		Total	
	No.	No./tp	No.	No./tp	No.	No./tp	No.	No./tp	No.	No./tp
Araneae	23	5.7	5	2.5	37	9.2	2	1.0	67	5.6
Acari	1	0.2	0	0.0	0	0.0	0	0.0	1	0.1
Collembola	2	0.5	1	0.5	1	0.2	0	0.0	4	0.3
Orthoptera	5	1.2	0	0.0	3	0.7	5	2.5	13	1.1
Isoptera	2	0.5	12	6.0	0	0.0	0	0.0	14	1.2
Embioptera	1	0.2	0	0.0	0	0.0	0	0.0	1	0.1
Hemiptera (Homo)	42	10.5	14	7.0	12	3.0	7	3.5	75	6.2
Hemiptera (Het)	8	2.0	3	1.5	7	1.7	8	4.0	26	2.2
Psocoptera	7	1.7	1	0.5	2	0.5	3	1.5	13	1.1
Hymenoptera	84	21.0	335	167.5	17	4.2	24	12.0	460	38.3
Coleoptera	46	11.5	17	8.5	17	4.2	11	5.5	91	7.6
Neuroptera	0	0.0	0	0.0	1	0.2	0	0.0	1	0.1
Strepsiptera	1	0.2	0	0.0	1	0.2	1	0.5	3	0.2
Diptera	1950	487.5	695	347.5	895	223.7	1170	585.0	4710	392.5
Lepidoptera	15	3.7	7	3.5	14	3.5	5	2.5	41	3.4
Total	2232	558.0	1110	555.0	1043	260.7	1236	618.0	5621	468.4

Table 4. Total Count Light Trap: 15 Meters

Group	13 Dec. 77		25 Mar. 78		12 Sept. 78		3 Oct. 78		Total	
	No.	No./tp	No.	No./tp	No.	No./tp	No.	No./tp	No.	No./tp
Araneae	2	0.5	0	0.0	6	1.5	1	1.0	9	0.8
Orthoptera	9	2.2	4	2.0	3	0.7	3	3.0	19	1.7
Isoptera	1	0.2	4	2.0	0	0.0	0	0.0	5	0.5
Hemiptera (Homo)	49	12.2	22	11.0	18	4.5	21	21.0	110	10.0
Hemiptera (Het)	34	8.5	9	4.5	7	1.7	11	11.0	61	5.5
Psocoptera	14	3.5	4	2.0	14	3.5	6	6.0	38	3.5
Hymenoptera	235	58.7	304	152.0	35	8.7	43	43.0	617	56.1
Coleoptera	153	38.2	35	17.5	29	7.2	27	27.0	244	22.2
Strepsiptera	1	0.2	0	0.0	2	0.5	2	2.0	5	0.5
Neuroptera	0	0.0	1	0.5	1	0.2	3	3.0	5	0.5
Diptera	6823	1705.7	2119	1059.5	3021	755.2	6489	6489.0	18452	1677.5
Lepidoptera	299	74.7	68	34.0	128	42.0	165	165.0	660	60.0
Total	7620	1905.0	2571	1285.5	3264	816.0	6771	6771.0	20226	1838.7

Table 5. Total Count Emergence Traps

Group	13 Dec. 77 No.	No./tp	25 Mar. 78 No.	No./tp	12 Sept. 78 No.	No./tp	3 Oct. 78 No.	No./tp	Total No.	No./tp
Araneae	78	6.5	51	2.1	76	2.8	41	1.5	246	2.7
Acari	87	7.2	0	0	87	3.2	132	4.9	306	3.4
Phalangida	0	0	0	0	0	0	1	0.0	1	0.0
Pseudoscorpionida	13	1.1	0	0	0	0	3	0.1	16	0.2
Scorpionida	1	0.1	0	0	1	0.0	1	0.0	3	0.0
Thelyphonida	1	0.1	0	0	0	0	0	0	1	0.0
Isopoda	2	0.2	0	0	0	0	3	0.1	5	0.1
Diplopoda	2	0.2	0	0	0	0	0	0	2	0.0
Chilopoda	2	0.2	0	0	0	0	0	0	2	0.0
Collembola	1118	93.2	434	18.1	474	17.6	383	14.2	2409	26.8
Microcoryphia	1	0.1	0	0	1	0.0	0	0	2	0.0
Thysanura	0	0	0	0	0	0	2	0.1	2	0.0
Orthoptera	22	1.8	14	0.6	23	0.9	12	0.4	71	0.8
Isoptera	6	0.5	2	0.1	2	0.1	100	3.7	110	1.2
Dermaptera	3	0.2	1	0.0	1	0.0	0	0	5	0.1
Embioptera	0	0	0	0	3	0.1	1	0.0	4	0.0
Hemiptera (Homo)	24	2.0	20	0.8	24	0.9	19	0.7	87	1.0
Hemiptera (Het)	22	1.8	15	0.6	19	0.7	10	0.4	66	0.7
Psocoptera	17	1.4	1	0.0	3	0.1	6	0.2	27	0.3
Thysanoptera	35	2.9	3	0.1	4	0.1	3	0.1	45	0.5
Hymenoptera	471	39.2	1932	80.5	292	10.8	188	7.0	2883	32.0
Coleoptera	452	37.7	456	19.0	436	16.1	603	22.3	1947	21.6
Diptera	1479	123.2	1559	65.0	874	32.4	566	21.0	4478	48.8
Lepidoptera	7	0.6	18	0.7	31	1.1	9	0.3	65	0.7
Total	3843	320.2	4506	187.8	2351	87.1	2083	77.1	12783	142.0

Table 6. Total Count Flight Trap

Group	13 Dec. 77 No.	No./tp	25 Mar. 78 No.	No./tp	12 Sept. 78 No.	No./tp	3 Oct. 78 No.	No./tp	Total No.	No./tp
Araneae	4	4	11	11	15	15	14	14	40	13.3
Acari	7	7	—	—	8	8	—	—	8	2.7
Collembola	16	16	37	37	4	4	1	1	42	14.0
Microcoryphia	2	2	1	1	3	3	6	6	10	3.3
Odonata	—	—	—	—	—	—	1	1	1	0.3
Orthoptera	13	13	41	41	52	52	60	60	153	51.0
Isoptera	2	2	5	5	—	—	11	11	16	5.3
Hemiptera (Homo)	14	14	55	55	102	102	109	109	266	88.7
Hemiptera (Het)	—	—	24	24	18	18	8	8	50	16.7
Psocoptera	4	4	27	27	54	54	19	19	100	33.3
Thysanoptera	1	1	—	—	—	—	—	—	1	0.3
Hymenoptera	28	28	823	823	723	723	1212	1212	2758	919.3
Coleoptera	18	18	200	200	191	191	208	208	599	199.6
Neuroptera	7	7	7	7	4	4	4	4	15	5.0
Diptera	536	536	11550	11550	3825	3825	4934	4934	20309	6769.7
Trichoptera	—	—	7	7	5	5	1	1	13	4.3
Lepidoptera	50	50	248	248	426	426	297	297	971	323.7
	745	745	13132	13132	5729	5729	6885	6885	25746	8582.0

Table 7. Total Count Pitfall Traps

Group	13 Dec. 77		25 Mar. 78		12 Sept. 78		3 Oct. 78		Total	
	No.	No./tp	No.	No./tp	No.	No./tp	No.	No./tp	No.	No./tp
Araneae	45	2.2	24	1.2	23	1.1	30	1.5	122	1.5
Acari	4249	212.4	1048	52.4	2845	142.2	1378	68.9	9520	119.0
Pseudoscorpionida	7	0.3	0	0	0	0	5	0.4	12	0.1
Thelyphonida	2	0.1	0	0	0	0	0	0	2	0.0
Isopoda	1	0.0	0	0	0	0	5	0.4	6	0.1
Diplopoda	2	0.1	0	0	0	0	1	0.0	3	0.0
Collembola	2123	106.1	945	47.2	1642	82.1	2216	110.8	6926	86.6
Microcoryphia	2	0.1	0	0	3	0.1	1	0.0	6	0.1
Orthoptera	92	4.6	98	4.9	45	2.2	73	3.6	308	3.8
Isoptera	5	0.2	0	0	8	0.4	0	0	13	0.2
Dermaptera	130	6.5	45	2.2	11	0.5	33	1.6	219	2.7
Hemiptera (Hm)	0	0	0	0	1	0.0	3	0.1	4	0.0
Hemiptera (Ht)	66	3.3	13	0.6	22	1.1	34	1.7	135	1.7
Psocoptera	1	0.0	1	0.0	0	0	1	0.0	3	0.0
Thysanoptera	0	0	0	0	11	0.5	6	0.3	17	0.2
Hymenoptera	1745	87.2	638	31.9	1024	51.2	1355	67.7	4762	59.5
Coleoptera	4350	217.5	2842	142.1	2499	124.9	3912	195.6	13603	170.0
Diptera	5840	292.0	5044	252.2	2495	124.7	5120	256.0	18499	231.2
Lepidoptera	1	0.0	0	0	0	0	3	0.1	4	0.0
Total	18661	933.0	10690	534.5	10629	531.4	14176	708.8	54156	676.9

Table 8.   Biomass Count Light Trap: 1 Meter
(total 2 traps)

Group	Weight (gms.)	Percentage
Coleoptera	0.0621	42.68
Elateridae	0.0615	42.27
Platypodidae	0.0006	0.41
Diptera	0.0418	28.04
Culicidae	0.0151	10.38
Others	0.0257	17.66
Orthoptera	0.0312	21.44
Blattoidea	0.0230	15.67
Gryllidae	0.0082	5.64
Lepidoptera	0.0082	5.64
Hemiptera	0.0008	0.55
Dipsocoridae	0.0003	0.21
Cicadellidae	0.0002	0.14
Derbidae	0.0002	0.14
Achilidae	0.0001	0.07
Psocoptera	0.0001	0.07
Hymenoptera	0.0023	1.58
Total	0.1455	100.00

Table 9. Biomass Count Light Trap: 15 meters
(total 1 trap)

Group	Weight (gms.)	Percentage
Lepidoptera	0.2159	52.76
Diptera	0.1345	32.87
Culicidae	0.0034	0.83
Others	0.1311	32.04
Hymenoptera	0.0453	11.07
Formicidae	0.0221	5.40
Others	0.0232	5.67
Coleoptera	0.0091	2.22
Curculionidae	0.0050	1.22
Chrysomelidae	0.0024	0.59
Lycidae	0.0016	0.39
Erotylidae	0.0001	0.02
Orthoptera	0.0019	0.46
Blattoidea	0.0010	0.24
Gryllidae	0.0009	0.22
Hemiptera	0.0012	0.29
Miridae	0.0008	0.20
Cicadellidae	0.0004	0.10
Neuroptera	0.0012	0.29
Chrysopidae	0.0009	0.22
Sisyridae	0.0003	0.07
Strepsiptera	0.0001	0.02
Total	0.4092	100.00

Table 10. *Biomass Count Flight Trap*

Group	Weight (gms.)	Percentage
Diptera	6.0901	49.33
Tabanidae	4.6489	37.66
Micropezidae	0.0366	0.30
Others	1.4046	11.38
Hymenoptera	2.0783	16.83
Formicidae	0.3387	2.74
Megachilidae	0.1837	1.49
Apidae	0.0727	0.59
Halictidae	0.0093	0.08
Others	1.4739	11.94
Coleoptera	1.4832	12.01
Cerambycidae	0.8149	6.60
Chrysomelidae	0.1663	1.35
Elateridae	0.1334	1.08
Phengodidae	0.0939	0.76
Tenebrionidae	0.0554	0.45
Curculionidae	0.0437	0.35
Eucnemidae	0.0412	0.33
Staphylinidae	0.0316	0.26
Mordellidae	0.0202	0.16
Oedemeridae	0.0193	0.16
Erotylidae	0.0134	0.11
Scaphidiidae	0.0116	0.09
Nitidulidae	0.0088	0.07
Platypodidae	0.0076	0.06
Carabidae	0.0062	0.05
Coccinellidae	0.0046	0.04
Lampyridae	0.0025	0.02
Ptilodactylidae	0.0022	0.02
Cantharidae	0.0021	0.02
Leptodiridae	0.0016	0.01
Melandryidae	0.0012	0.01
Buprestidae	0.0011	0.01
Anobiidae	0.0010	0.01
Lycidae	0.0008	0.01
Scolytidae	0.0002	trace
Orthoptera	1.2917	10.46
Acrididae	0.7005	5.67
Blattoidea	0.4309	3.49
Tettigoniidae	0.0675	0.55
Gryllidae	0.0645	0.52
Tetrigidae	0.0200	0.16

Table 10.   Continued

Group	Weight (gms.)	Percentage
Mantoidea	0.0077	0.06
Phasmoidea	0.0006	trace
Lepidoptera	1.0290	8.34
Hemiptera	0.1862	1.50
Cicadellidae	0.0587	0.48
Issidae	0.0283	0.23
Cixiidae	0.0262	0.21
Coreidae	0.0243	0.20
Achilixiidae	0.0148	0.12
Achilidae	0.0083	0.07
Derbidae	0.0074	0.06
Nabidae	0.0050	0.04
Lygaeidae	0.0049	0.04
Cydnidae	0.0045	0.04
Miridae	0.0015	0.01
Tingidae	0.0008	0.01
Psyllidae	0.0006	trace
Aleyrodidae	0.0005	trace
Anthocoridae	0.0004	trace
Isoptera	0.1330	1.08
Araneae	0.0230	0.19
Odonata	0.0079	0.06
Neuroptera	0.0064	0.05
Psocoptera	0.0017	0.01
Collembola	0.0005	trace
Trichoptera	0.0005	trace
Total	12.3443	100.00

Table 11.   Biomass Count Emergence Traps (27 traps)

Group	Weight (gms.)	Percentage
Coleoptera	0.2401	37.38
Scolytidae	0.1271	19.79
Scydmaenidae	0.0081	1.26
Staphylinidae	0.0115	1.79
Chrysomelidae	0.0209	3.25
Curculionidae	0.0349	5.43
Cantharidae	0.0001	0.02

Table 11. Continued

Group	Weight (gms.)	Percentage
Elateridae	0.0057	0.89
Mordellidae	0.0013	0.20
Platypodidae	0.0021	0.33
Pselaphidae	0.0046	0.72
Lampyridae	0.0150	2.34
Leiodidae	0.0037	0.58
Nitidulidae	0.0006	0.09
Eucnemidae	0.0015	0.23
Lathridiidae	0.0008	0.12
?	0.0022	0.34
Isoptera	0.1051	16.36
Hymenoptera	0.0731	11.38
Formicidae	0.0499	7.77
Others	0.0232	3.61
Araneae	0.0641	9.98
Diptera	0.0388	6.04
Collembola	0.0331	5.15
Hemiptera	0.0239	3.72
Cicadellidae	0.0055	0.86
Cercopidae	0.0060	0.93
Cixiidae	0.0056	0.87
Schizopteridae	0.0048	0.75
Delphacidae	0.0006	0.09
Lygaeidae	0.0004	0.06
Orthoptera	0.0196	3.05
Blattoidea	0.0097	1.51
Gryllidae	0.0099	1.54
Acari	0.0208	3.24
Lepidoptera	0.0077	1.20
Isopoda	0.0053	0.83
Psocoptera	0.0046	0.72
Thysanoptera	0.0019	0.30
Pseudoscorpionida	0.0018	0.28
Phalangida	0.0017	0.26
Embioptera	0.0007	0.11
Total	0.6423	100.00

Table 12. Biomass Count Feces-Picric Acid Pitfall
Traps (5 traps)

Groups	Weight	Percentage
Coleoptera	15.4285	95.98
Scarabaeidae	15.3265	95.35
Staphylinidae	0.0506	0.31
Leiodidae (Catopinae)	0.0453	0.28
Ptiliidae	0.0035	0.02
Histeridae	0.0011	0.01
Scolytidae	0.0007	trace
Hydrophilidae	0.0006	trace
Hymenoptera	0.3860	2.40
Formicidae	0.3857	2.40
Others	0.0003	trace
Orthoptera	0.0783	0.49
Blattoidea	0.0367	0.23
Gryllidae	0.0416	0.26
Diptera	0.0732	0.45
Acari	0.0641	0.40
Hemiptera	0.0153	0.10
Cydnidae	0.0146	0.09
Cixiidae	0.0007	trace
Araneae	0.0098	0.06
Dermaptera	0.0086	0.05
Collembola	0.0055	0.03
Lepidoptera	0.0048	0.03
Total	16.0741	100.00

Table 13.   Biomass Count
Feces—Chloral Hydrate Pitfall Trap (5 traps)

Group	Weight	Percentage
Coleoptera	2.0748	77.71
Scarabaeidae	1.9319	72.36
Staphylinidae	0.0606	2.27
Leiodidae (Catopinae)	0.0574	2.15
Ptiliidae	0.0077	0.29
Histeridae	0.0075	0.28
Hydrophilidae	0.0048	0.18
Scolytidae	0.0032	0.12
Nitidulidae	0.0017	0.06
Orthoptera	0.4088	15.31
Blattoidea	0.0423	1.58
Gryllidae	0.3665	13.73
Diptera	0.0910	3.41
Micropezidae	0.0041	0.15
Others	0.0869	3.25
Dermaptera	0.0372	1.39
Hymenoptera	0.0194	0.73
Formicidae	0.0162	0.61
Others	0.0032	0.12
Acari	0.0165	0.62
Collembola	0.0080	0.30
Araneae	0.0070	0.26
Hemiptera	0.0034	0.13
Schizopteridae (sclerotized)	0.0019	0.07
Schizopteridae (not scl.)	0.0010	0.04
Dipsocoridae	0.0005	0.02
Isopoda	0.0020	0.07
Pseudoscorpionida	0.0018	0.07
Total	2.6699	100.00

Appendix Tables

Table 14. Biomass Count
Fish—Picric Acid Pitfall Traps (5 traps)

Group	Weight	Percentage
Coleoptera	2.6138	67.46
Scarabaeidae	2.4612	63.52
Leiodidae (Catopinae)	0.0769	1.98
Staphylinidae	0.0559	1.44
Hydrophilidae	0.0135	0.35
Pselaphidae	0.0021	0.05
Scolytidae	0.0020	0.05
Ptiliidae	0.0016	0.04
Histeridae	0.0006	0.02
Orthoptera	0.6817	17.59
Blattoidea	0.2391	6.17
Gryllidae	0.4426	11.42
Hymenoptera	0.3290	8.49
Formicidae	0.2887	7.45
Apidae	0.0370	0.95
Others	0.0033	0.08
Diptera	0.1346	3.47
Dermaptera	0.0332	0.86
Acari	0.0272	0.70
Hemiptera	0.0188	0.49
Reduviidae	0.0080	0.21
Cicadellidae	0.0040	0.10
Achilidae	0.0033	0.09
Dipsocoridae	0.0025	0.06
Schizopteridae	0.0010	0.03
Araneae	0.0195	0.50
Lepidoptera	0.0072	0.19
Psocoptera	0.0034	0.09
Thysanoptera	0.0013	0.03
Pseudoscorpionida	0.0002	0.01
Total	3.8746	100.00

Table 15.   Biomass Count
Fish—Chloral Hydrate Pitfall Traps (5 traps)

Group	Weight	Percentage
Coleoptera	2.6021	75.47
Scarabaeidae	2.4937	72.32
Scolytidae	0.0488	1.42
Staphylinidae	0.0329	0.95
Hydrophilidae	0.0182	0.44
Histeridae	0.0033	0.10
Ptiliidae	0.0052	0.15
Orthoptera	0.4640	13.46
Blattoidea	0.2006	5.82
Gryllidae	0.2634	7.64
Hymenoptera	0.2226	6.46
Formicidae	0.1946	5.64
Apidae	0.0189	0.55
Others	0.0091	0.26
Diptera	0.0613	1.78
Dermaptera	0.0262	0.76
Araneae	0.0259	0.75
Acari	0.0119	0.35
Collembola	0.0116	0.34
Hemiptera (Dipsocoridae)	0.0045	0.13
Isopoda	0.0044	0.13
Thysanura	0.0041	0.12
Pseudoscorpionida	0.0043	0.12
Diplopoda	0.0028	0.08
Total	3.4480	100.00

Table 16. Numbers of Hemiptera Encountered In Reserva Ducke By Trap

Family	1 m.	%	15 m.	%	Flight	%	Emergence	%	Baited Pitfall	%	Total	%
Acanalonidae	—	—	1	0.04	—	—	—	—	—	—	1	0.01
Achilidae	21	1.67	72	2.61	130	3.83	99	4.57	—	—	322	2.95
Achilixiidae	5	0.40	10	0.36	239	7.03	12	0.55	2	0.15	268	2.45
Aethalionidae	—	—	1	0.04	3	0.09	—	—	—	—	4	0.04
Aleyrodidae	9	0.72	112	4.06	2	0.06	—	—	—	—	123	1.13
Cercopidae	8	0.64	3	0.11	11	0.32	49	2.26	1	0.07	72	0.66
Cicadellidae	192	15.26	562	20.36	1219	35.87	335	15.47	10	0.74	2318	21.22
Cicadidae	—	—	—	—	—	—	1	0.05	—	—	1	0.01
Cixiidae	40	3.18	152	5.51	456	13.42	703	32.47	2	0.15	1353	12.38
Delphacidae	1	0.08	9	0.33	23	0.68	76	3.51	—	—	109	1.00
Derbidae	713	56.68	496	17.97	600	17.66	117	5.40	1	0.07	1927	17.63
Dictyopharidae	2	0.15	1	0.04	12	0.35	—	—	—	—	15	0.14
Flatidae	2	0.15	16	0.58	10	0.29	—	—	—	—	28	0.26
Fulgoridae	—	—	—	—	2	0.06	—	—	—	—	2	0.02
Issidae	—	—	1	0.04	23	0.68	—	—	—	—	24	0.22
Lophopidae	—	—	—	—	1	0.03	—	—	—	—	1	0.01
Membracidae	1	0.08	—	—	17	0.50	—	—	—	—	18	0.17

	n	%	n	%	n	%	n	%	n	%	n	%
Monophlebiidae	—	—	—	—	1	0.03	—	—	—	—	1	0.01
Nogodinidae	—	—	—	—	9	0.26	—	—	—	—	9	0.08
Psyllidae	—	—	5	0.18	95	2.80	—	—	—	—	100	0.92
Tropiduchidae	—	—	1	0.04	2	0.06	—	—	—	—	3	0.03
Alydidae	—	—	1	0.04	1	0.03	—	—	—	—	2	0.02
Anthocoridae	12	0.95	3	0.11	—	—	45	2.08	66	4.90	126	1.15
Aradidae	—	—	—	—	1	0.03	2	0.09	—	—	3	0.03
Cydnidae	45	3.58	—	—	124	3.65	4	0.18	296	21.97	424	3.88
Dipsocoridae	3	0.24	—	—	5	0.15	243	11.22	600	44.54	893	8.17
Enicocephalidae	1	0.08	—	—	—	—	4	0.18	—	—	7	0.06
Lygaeidae	—	—	5	0.18	91	2.68	41	1.89	1	0.07	139	1.27
Mesoveliidae	—	—	1	0.04	—	—	—	—	—	—	1	0.01
Miridae	17	1.35	191	6.92	263	7.74	19	0.88	3	0.22	493	4.51
Nabidae	—	—	1	0.04	11	0.32	—	—	—	—	12	0.11
Pentatomidae	—	—	—	—	2	0.06	—	—	—	—	2	0.02
Reduviidae	47	3.74	38	1.38	39	1.15	14	0.65	7	0.52	145	1.33
Schizopteridae	136	10.81	1078	39.06	2	0.06	395	18.24	357	26.50	1968	18.01
Scutellaridae	—	—	—	—	1	0.03	—	—	—	—	1	0.01
Tingidae	3	0.24	—	—	3	0.09	6	0.28	1	0.07	13	0.12
Total	1258		2760		3398		2165		1347		10.928	

Table 17.   Number of Neuroptera Encountered In Resrva Ducke By Trap

Family	Light 1 m.	%	Light 15 m.	%	Flight	%	Emergence	%	Baited Pitfall	%	Total	%
Ascalaphidae	—	—	—	—	—	—	—	—	2	100.00	2	0.80
Chrysopidae	4	40.00	34	49.28	112	66.67	—	—	—	—	150	59.76
Coniopterygidae	—	—	4	5.80	4	2.38	1	50.00	—	—	9	3.59
Dilaridae	—	—	19	27.54	—	—	—	—	—	—	19	7.57
Hemerobiidae	5	50.00	3	4.35	—	—	—	—	—	—	8	3.19
Mantispidae	1	10.00	7	10.14	50	29.76	1	50.00	—	—	59	23.51
Myrmeleontidae	—	—	1	1.45	2	1.19	—	—	—	—	3	1.20
Sisyridae	—	—	1	1.45	—	—	—	—	—	—	1	0.40
Total	10		69		168		2		2		251	100.02

Table 18. Number of Coleoptera Encountered In Reserva Ducke By Trap

Family	Light 1 m.	%	Light 15 m.	%	Flight	%	Emergence	%	Baited Pitfall	%	Total	%
Alleculidae	1	0.09	3	0.07	32	0.43	21	0.08	—	—	57	0.02
Anobiidae	7	0.64	37	0.85	30	0.40	27	0.11	—	—	101	0.04
Anthicidae	5	0.46	18	0.41	—	—	3	0.01	—	—	26	0.01
Anthribidae	1	0.09	—	—	35	0.47	1	—	1	—	37	0.01
Biphyllidae	3	0.27	1	0.02	—	—	1	—	—	—	6	—
Bostrichidae	1	0.09	2	0.05	—	—	1	—	—	—	4	—
Brentidae	—	—	12	0.27	7	0.09	—	—	—	—	19	0.01
Bruchidae	—	—	2	0.05	3	0.04	1	—	—	—	6	—
Buprestidae	—	—	2	0.05	25	0.34	1	—	—	—	28	0.01
Byrrhidae	3	0.27	4	0.09	—	—	—	—	—	—	7	—
Cantharidae	30	2.73	14	0.32	158	2.13	85	0.34	—	—	287	0.11
Carabidae	11	1.00	82	1.88	450	6.06	74	0.30	22	0.01	639	0.25
Cerambycidae	—	—	13	0.30	189	2.54	3	0.01	1	—	206	0.08
Chelonariidae	1	0.09	7	0.16	1	0.01	1	—	—	—	10	—
Chrysomelidae	62	5.66	341	7.81	1213	16.33	1203	4.83	33	0.02	2852	1.11
Cisidae	—	—	2	0.05	—	—	3	0.01	—	—	5	—
Cleridae	—	—	1	0.02	23	0.31	1	—	—	—	25	0.01
Coccinellidae	2	0.18	4	0.09	106	1.43	3	0.01	—	—	115	0.04
Colydiidae	2	0.18	13	0.30	4	0.05	7	0.03	11	—	37	0.01
Cryptophagidae	5	0.46	15	0.34	1	0.01	4	0.02	1	—	26	0.01
Cucujidae	12	1.09	34	0.78	2	0.03	15	0.06	1	—	64	0.02
Curculionidae	36	3.28	81	1.86	548	7.38	225	0.90	4	—	894	0.35
Dascillidae	—	—	—	—	123	1.66	13	0.05	—	—	136	0.05

Table 18. Continued

Family	Light 1 m.	%	Light 15 m.	%	Flight	%	Emergence	%	Baited Pitfall	%	Total	%
Dermestidae	—	—	2	0.05	3	0.04	25	0.10	—	—	30	0.01
Dryopidae	—	—	—	—	—	—	1	—	—	—	1	—
Dytiscidae	—	—	2	0.05	11	0.15	2	0.01	3	—	18	0.01
Elateridae	59	5.38	8	0.18	1011	13.61	81	0.33	1	—	1160	0.45
Endomychidae	2	0.18	17	0.39	36	0.48	26	0.10	—	—	81	0.03
Erotylidae	10	0.91	67	1.53	118	1.59	5	0.02	—	—	200	0.08
Eucnemidae	1	0.09	50	1.15	165	2.22	5	0.02	—	—	221	0.09
Euglenidae	10	0.91	79	1.81	16	2.22	23	0.09	—	—	128	0.05
Helodidae	—	—	1	0.02	34	0.46	—	—	—	—	35	0.01
Histeridae	1	0.09	—	—	—	—	95	0.38	2339	1.07	2435	0.95
Hydrophilidae	1	0.09	—	—	—	—	22	0.09	5863	2.68	5886	2.30
Lagriidae	1	0.09	3	0.07	31	0.42	6	0.02	—	—	41	0.02
Lampyridae	5	0.46	33	0.76	97	1.31	31	0.12	—	—	166	0.06
Languriidae	—	—	3	0.07	—	—	—	—	—	—	3	—
Lathridiidae	3	0.27	17	0.39	—	—	5	0.02	2	—	27	0.01
Leiodidae	5	0.46	1	0.02	8	0.11	91	0.36	33	0.02	138	0.05
Leptodiridae	6	0.55	2	0.05	12	0.16	99	0.39	57737	26.41	57856	22.56
Limnichidae	—	—	1	0.02	—	—	—	—	—	—	1	—
Lycidae	8	0.73	97	2.22	66	0.89	7	0.03	1	—	179	0.07
Lymexylonidae	—	—	3	0.07	9	0.12	—	—	—	—	12	—
Melandryidae	9	0.82	4	0.09	70	0.94	21	0.08	—	—	104	0.04
Meloidae	1	0.09	—	—	7	0.09	1	—	—	—	9	—
Monommidae	2	0.18	3	0.07	46	0.62	3	0.01	—	—	54	0.02
Mordellidae	5	0.46	3	0.07	765	10.30	17	0.07	—	—	790	0.31

Family	No.	%	No.	%	No.	%	No.	%	No.	%	No.	%
Mycetophagidae	10	0.91	36	0.82	5	0.07	10	0.04	—	—	61	0.02
Nitidulidae	2	0.18	41	0.94	270	3.63	121	0.49	154	0.07	588	0.23
Nosodendiridae	—	—	—	—	—	—	1	—	—	—	1	—
Noteridae	—	—	—	—	—	—	1	—	—	—	1	—
Oedemeridae	—	—	25	0.57	34	0.46	1	—	—	—	60	0.02
Orthoperidae	13	1.19	69	1.58	—	—	10	0.04	6	—	98	0.04
Ostomidae	1	0.09	—	—	2	0.03	1	—	—	—	4	—
Passalidae	—	—	2	0.05	—	—	—	—	—	—	2	—
Pedilidae	—	—	—	—	2	0.03	2	0.01	—	—	4	—
Phalacridae	—	—	7	0.16	—	—	1	—	—	—	8	—
Phengodidae	11	1.00	—	—	150	2.02	10	0.04	—	—	171	0.07
Platypodae	43	3.92	172	3.94	204	2.75	51	0.20	—	—	470	9.18
Pselaphidae	101	9.22	41	0.94	2	0.03	946	3.80	173	0.08	1263	0.49
Ptiliidae	—	—	—	—	—	—	531	2.13	36708	16.79	37239	14.52
Ptilodactylidae	6	0.55	11	0.25	218	2.93	29	0.12	—	—	264	0.10
Rhipiphoridae	3	0.27	—	—	10	0.13	—	—	—	—	13	0.01
Rhipoceridae	—	—	—	—	10	0.13	1	—	—	—	11	—
Rhizophariidae	—	—	—	—	1	0.01	9	0.04	—	—	10	—
Salpingidae	1	0.09	3	0.07	4	0.05	—	—	—	—	8	—
Scaphidiidae	—	—	1	0.02	111	1.49	26	0.10	13	0.01	151	0.06
Scarabaeidae	185	16.88	10	0.23	32	0.43	82	0.33	19300	8.83	19609	7.65
Scolytidae	70	6.39	331	7.58	13	0.17	15875	63.70	575	0.26	16864	6.58
Scydmaenidae	123	11.22	56	1.28	1	0.01	1393	5.59	27	0.01	1600	0.62
Staphylinidae	192	17.52	2436	55.81	879	11.83	3470	13.92	95633	43.74	102610	40.01
Tenebrionidae	17	1.55	19	0.44	21	0.28	89	0.36	9	—	155	0.06
Throscidae	7	0.64	21	0.48	5	0.07	4	0.02	—	—	37	0.01
Total	1096	99.96	4365	100.01	7429	99.90	24923	99.93	218651	100.00	256464	99.93

BIBLIOGRAPHY

All journal abbreviations are in accordance with *World List of Scientific Periodicals*.

Adams, P. A. 1970. A review of the New World Dilaridae. *Postilla*, no. 148.
Adis, J. 1979a. Vergleichende okologische Studien an der terrestrischen Arthropodenfauna Zentralamazonischer Überschwemmungswälder. (Ph.D. dissertation presented to Fakultät für Naturwissenschaften und Mathematik der Universität Ulm, West Germany.)
Adis, J. 1979b. Problems of interpreting arthropod samplings with pitfall traps. *Zool. Ang.* 202(314):177–184.
Araujo, R. L. 1977. *Catálogo dos Isoptera do Novo Mundo*. Academia Brasileira de Ciências. Rio de Janeiro.
Bandeira, A. G. 1979. Ecologia de cupins (Insecta: Isoptera) da Amazônia Central: efeitos do desmatamento sobre as populações. *Acta Amaz.* 9(3):481–499.
Bates, H. W. 1962. (reprint edition). *The Naturalist on the River Amazons*. Berkeley: University of California Press.
Beck, L. 1968. Sôbre a biologia de alguns Aracnídeos na floresta tropical da Reserva Ducke (I.N.P.A., Manaus/Brasil). *Amazoniana* 1(3):247–250.
Beck, L. 1970. Zur Ökologie der Bodenarthropoden im Regenwaldgebiet des Amazonasbeckens. *Habititationsschrift*. Ruhr-Universität Bochum.
Beck, L. 1971. Bodenzoologische Gliederung und Charakterisierung des amazonischen Regenwaldes. *Amazoniana* 3:69–132.
Beck, L. and Schubart, H. 1968. Revision der Gattung *Cryptocellus* Westwood 1874. (Arachnida: Ricinuclei). *Senckenbergiana biol.* 49(1):67–78.
Beebe, W. 1916. Fauna of four square feet of jungle debris. *Zoologica, N.Y. Zoological Soc.* 2(4):107–119.
Berthet, P. 1963. Mesure de la consommation d'oxygène des Oribatides (Acariens) de la litière des forêts. In J. Doeksen and J. van der Drift, *Soil Organisms*. Amsterdam. Pp. 18–31.
Bigger, M. 1976. Oscillations of tropical insect populations. *Nature* 259:207–209.

Brach, V. 1978. *Brachynemurus nebulosus* (Neuroptera: Myrmeleontidae): a possible Batesian mimic of Florida mutillid wasps (Hymenoptera: Mutillidae). *Ent. News* 89:153–156.

Brinkmann, W. L. F. 1971. Light environment in tropical rain forest of Central Amazonia. *Acta Amaz.* 1(2):37–48.

Briscoe, C. B. 1960. The early results of mycorrhiza inoculation of pine in Puerto Rico. *Caribbean Forester* 20:73.

Brown, K. S., Jr. 1977. Centros de evolução, refúgios quaternários e conservação de patrimônios genéticos na região neotropical: padrões de diferenciação em Ithomiinae (Lepidoptera: Nymphalidae). *Acta Amaz.* 7(1):75–137.

Brown, W. L., Jr. 1973. A comparison of the Hylean and Congo-West African Rain Forest ant Faunas, In B. J. Meggers, E. S. Ayensu, and D. Duckworth. *Tropical Forest Ecosystems in Africa and South America: A Comparative Review*, pp. 161–185. Washington, D.C.: Smithsonian Institution Press.

Brues, C. T., A. L. Melander, and F. M. Carpenter. 1954. Classification of Insects. *Bull. Mus. comp. Zool., Harvard Univ.* 108:1–917.

Carpenter, F. M. 1930. The Lower Permian Insects of Kansas. Part 1. Introduction and the Order Mecoptera. *Bull. Mus. comp. Zool., Harvard Univ.* 70:69–101.

Carvalho, J. C. M. 1957–1960. A catalogue of the Miridae of the World. *Archos Mus. nac., Rio de J.*, 5 vols.

Costa, C. 1975. Systematics and evolution of the tribes Pyrophorini and Heligmini, with description of Campyloxeninae, new subfamily (Coleoptera, Elateridae). *Archos Zool. Est. S Paulo* 26(2):49–190.

Dammerman, K. W. 1938. Second contribution to a study of the tropical soil and surface fauna. *Treubia* 16(1):121–147.

Drift, J. van der. 1963. A comparative study of the soil fauna in forests and cultivated land on sandy soils in Suriname. *Stud. fauna Suriname* 6(32):1–42.

Edmonds, G. F., Jr., S. L. Jensen, and L. Berner. 1976. *The Mayflies of North and Central America*. Minneapolis: University of Minnesota Press.

Emsley, M. G. 1969. The Schizopteridae (Hemiptera: Heteroptera) with the description of new species from Trinidad. *Mem. Am. ent. Soc.* 25:1–154.

Erwin, T. L. 1981. Taxon pulses, vicariance, and dispersal: An evolutionary synthesis illustrated by carabid beetles. In G. Nelson and D. E. Rosen, eds., *Vicariance Biogeography: A Critique*, pp. 159–196. New York: Columbia University Press.

Erwin, T. L. and J. Adis. (in press). Amazonian inundation forests:

Their role as short-term refuges and generators of species diversity and taxon pulses. In G. T. Prance, ed., *Biological Diversification in the Tropics.* New York: Columbia University Press.

Fairchild, G. B. 1968. Family Tabanidae. In N. Papavero, *A Catalogue of Diptera of the Americas South of the United States.* São Paulo: Universidade de São Paulo Press.

Fairchild, G. B. and D. G. Young. 1973. Studies of Phlebotomine sand flies. Annual Report. U.S. Army Medical Research and Development Command, Washington.

Falesi, I., B. N. Rodrigues da Silva, et al. 1969. *Os solos da área Manaus—Itacoatiara.* Série Estudados e Ensaios No. 1. Secretaria de Produção do Amazonas. IPEAN, Belém, Pará.

Fennah, R. G. 1954. The higher classification of the family Issidae (Homoptera: Fulgoroidea) with descriptions of new species. *Trans. R. ent. Soc. Lond.* 105(19):455–474, 15 figs.

Fittkau, E. J. and H. Klinge. 1973. On biomass and trophic structure of the Central Amazonian rain forest ecosystem. *Biotropica* 5(1):2–14.

Flint, O. S., Jr. 1971. Studies of Neotropical Caddisflies, XII: Rhyacophilidae, Glossosomatidae, Philopotamidae, and Psychomyiidae from the Amazon Basin (Trichoptera). *Amazoniana* (Kiel). 3(1):1–67.

Flint, O. S., Jr. 1974. The Trichoptera of Surinam. *Stud. fauna Suriname,* 14(55):1–151.

Flint, O. S., Jr. 1978. Studies of Neotropical Caddisflies, XXII: Hydropsychidae of the Amazon Basin (Trichoptera). *Amazoniana* (Kiel). 6(3):373–421.

Franken, W. 1979. Untersuchungen im Einzugsgebiet des zentralamazonischen Urwaldbaches "Barro Branco" auf der "terra firme." I. Abflussverhalten des Baches. *Amazoniana* (Kiel). 6(4):459–466.

Froeschner, R. C. 1960. Cydnidae of the Western Hemisphere. *Proc. U.S. natn. Mus.* 111:337–680.

Funke, W. 1971. M. food and energy turnover of leaf-eating insects and their influence on primary production. In H. Ellenberg, *Ecological Studies. Analysis and Synthesis,* 2:81–93.

Gibbs, R. J. 1967. The geochemistry of the Amazon River System. Part 1. The factors that control the salinity and the composition and concentration of the suspended solids. *Bull. geol. Soc. Am.* 78:1203–1232.

Gist, C. S. and D. A. Crossley, Jr. 1975. The litter arthropod community in a southern Appalachian hardwood forest: numbers, biomass and mineral element content. *Am. midl. Nat.* 93(1):107–122.

Goodland, R. J. and H. S. Irwin. 1977. Amazon forest and Cerrado: Development and environmental conservation. In G. T. Prance, and T. S. Elias, *Extinction Is Forever*, pp. 214–233. New York: New York Botanical Garden.

Goodnight, C. J. and M. L. Goodnight. 1956. Some observations in a tropical rain forest in Chiapas, Mexico. *Ecology* 37(1):139–150.

Greenslade, P. J. M. and P. Greenslade. 1967. Soil and litter fauna densities in the Solomon Islands. *Pedobiologia* 7(4):362–370.

Grimm, R., W. Funke, and J. Schauerman. 1974. Minimalprogram zur Ökosystemanalyse: Untersuchungen und Tierpopulationen in Wald-ökosystemen. *Verh. Ges. Ökologie*: 77–87.

Gruner, L. 1975. Ètude de l'activité des adultes de divers scarabeides antillais au moyen de plégeages lumineux et chimiques. *Ann. zool.-ecol. anim.* 7(3):399–423.

Haffer, J. 1969. Speciation in Amazonian forest birds. *Science, N.Y.* 165:131–137.

Hale, W. G. 1966. A population study of moorland Collembola. *Pedobiologia* 6:65–99.

Howden, H. F. and V. G. Nealis. 1975. Effects of clearing in a tropical rain forest on the composition of the coprophagous scarab beetle fauna (Coleoptera). *Biotropica* 7(2):77–83.

Irmler, U. 1977. Inundation-forest types in the vicinity of Manaus. *Biogeographica* 8:17–29.

Janzen, D. H. 1966. Coevolution of mutualism between ants and acacias in central America. *Evolution, Lancaster, Pa.* 20:249–275.

Janzen, D. H. 1971. Seed predation by animals. *Ann. Rev. Ecol. Syst.* 2:465–492.

Janzen, D. H. 1974. Tropical blackwater rivers, animals and mast fruiting by the Dipteracarpaceae. *Biotropica* 6(2):69–103.

Janzen, D. H. 1976. Why tropical trees have rotten cores. *Biotropica* 8:110.

Janzen, D. H. and C. M. Pond. 1975. A comparison by sweep sampling, of arthropod fauna of secondary vegetation in Michigan, England, and Costa Rica. *Trans. R. ent. Soc. Lond.* 127(1):33–50.

Kempf, W. W. 1972. Catálogo abreviado das formigas da Região Neotropical (Formicidae). *Studia ent.* 15(1/4):3–344.

Kitazawa, Y. 1967. Community metabolism of soil invertebrates in forest ecosystems in Japan. In K. Petrusewicz, *Secondary Productivity of Terrestrial Ecosystems*, pp. 649–661.

Klinge, H. 1972. Biomasa y materia orgánica del suelo en el ecosistema de la pluviselva centro-amazónica. Paper presented to IV Congresso Latino-Americano de la Ciencia del Suelo, Maracay, Venezuela, November 12–18, 1972.

Klinge, H. 1973. Struktur und Artenreichtum des zentral-amazon-ischen Regenwaldes. *Amazoniana* (Kiel). 4:283–292.

Klinge, H. and W. A. Rodrigues. 1968. Litter production in an area of Amazonian terra firme forest. I, II. *Amazoniana* (Kiel), 1:287–302.

Knight, K. L. and H. Stone. 1977. *A Catalog of the Mosquitoes of the World*. Baltimore, George W. King.

Kramer, J. P. 1976. Revision of the Neotropical planthoppers of the genus *Bladina* (Homoptera: Fulgoroidea: Nogodinidae). *Trans. Am. ent. Soc.* 102:1–40.

Kubitzki, K. 1977. The problem of rare and of frequent species: the monographer's view. In G. T. Prance and T. S. Elias, *Extinction Is Forever*, pp. 331–336. New York: New York Botanical Garden.

Lechthaler, R. 1956. Inventário das árvores de um hectare de terra firme da zona "Reserva Florestal Ducke" município de Manaus. *Amazônia* (Botanica), no. 3.

Leonard, M. D. 1928. A list of the Insects of New York. *Mem. Cornell Univ. ag. exp. Sta.* 101:1–1121.

Linsley, E. G. and J. W. MacSwain. 1955. Two new species of *Plega* from Mexico. *Pan-Pacif. Ent.* 31:15–19.

Lotka, A. J. 1945. In C. LeGros-Clarke, *Essays on Growth and Form*. Oxford: Oxford University Press.

McAtee, W. L. and J. R. Malloch. 1925. Revision of bugs of the family Cryptostemmatidae in the Collection of the United States National Museum. *Proc. U.S. natn. Mus.* 67:1–42, pls. 1–4.

Mahnert, V. 1979. Pseudoskorpione (Arachnida) aus dem Amazonas-Gebiet (Brasilien). *Revue suisse Zool.* 86(3):719–810.

Martins, A. V., P. Williams, and A. L. Falção. 1978. American sand flies. *Academia Brasileira de Ciencias*, Rio de Janeiro.

Martins, U. R. 1976. Sistemática e evolução da tribo Piezocerini (Coleoptera, Cerambycidae). *Archos Zool., Est. S Paulo* 27(3/4):165–370.

Meinander, M. 1972. A revision of the family Coniopterygidae (Planipennia). *Acta zool. fenn.* 136:1–357.

Meinander, M. 1973. Notes on some types of Enderlein's species of Coniopterygidae, with description of a new species of *Pampoconis* (Neuroptera). *Notul. ent.* 53:23–25.

Meinander, M. 1974. Coniopterygidae from South and Central America (Neuroptera). *Notul. ent.* 54:97–106.

Meinander, M. 1980. Coniopterygidae from Brazil (Neuroptera). *Ent. scand.* 11:129–144.

Metcalf, Z. P. 1936. *General Catalogue of the Hemiptera*. Smith College, Northhampton, Mass. Fasc. IV, part 2.

Metcalf, Z. P. 1943. *General Catalogue of the Hemiptera.* Smith College, Northhampton, Mass. Fasc. IV, part 3.

Metcalf, Z. P. 1945. *General Catalogue of the Hemiptera.* Smith College, Northhampton, Mass. Fasc. IV, part 4.

Metcalf, Z. P. 1946. *General Catalogue of the Hemiptera.* Smith College, Northhampton, Mass. Fasc. IV, part 8.

Metcalf, Z. P. 1947. *General Catalogue of the Hemiptera.* Smith College, Northhampton, Mass. Fasc. IV, part 9.

Metcalf, Z. P. 1954a. *General Catalogue of the Homoptera.* North Carolina State University, Raleigh, N.C. Fasc. IV, part 12.

Metcalf, Z. P. 1954b. *General Catalogue of the Homoptera.* North Carolina State University, Raleigh, N.C. Fasc. IV, part 14.

Metcalf, Z. P. 1955. *General Catalogue of the Homoptera.* North Carolina State University, Raleigh, N.C. Fasc. IV, part 17.

Metcalf, Z. P. 1957. *General Catalogue of the Homoptera.* North Carolina State University, Raleigh, N.C. Fasc. IV, part 13.

Metcalf, Z. P. 1958. *General Catalogue of the Homoptera.* North Carolina State University, Raleigh, N.C. Fasc. IV, part 15.

Metcalf, Z. P. 1963. *General Catalogue of the Homoptera.* North Carolina State University, Raleigh, N.C. Fasc. VIII, part 1, section 1.

Moore, H. E., Jr. 1973. The major groups of palms and their distribution. *Gentes Herb.*, 11:27–141.

New, T. R. 1980. Epipsocetae (Psocoptera) from the Reserva Ducke, Amazonas. *Acta Amaz.* 10(1):179–206.

Nicholson, T. and Rohter, L. 1979. Opening the Amazon. In *Newsweek*, January 5, 1979.

O'Brien, L. B. 1971. The systematics of the tribe Plectoderini in America north of Mexico. *Univ. Calif. Publs Ent.* 64:1–79, 157 figs.

Parker, F. D. and L. A. Stange. 1965. Systematic and biological notes on the tribe Platymantispini (Neuroptera: Mantispidae) and the description of a new species of *Plega* from Mexico. *Can. Ent.* 97:604–612.

Penny, N. D. 1977. Lista de Megaloptera, Neuroptera e Raphidioptera do México, América Central, ilhas Caraíbas e América do Sul. *Acta Amaz.* 7(4) suppl.

Penny, N. D. 1981a. Neuroptera of the Amazon Basin. Part 1. Sisyridae. *Acta Amaz.*

Penny, N. D. 1981b. Neuroptera of the Amazon Basin. Part 3. Ascalaphidae. *Acta Amaz.*

Penny, N. D. and G. W. Byers. 1979. A check-list of the Mecoptera of the World. *Acta Amaz.* 9(2):365–388.

Penny, N. D. and G. W. Byers. In preparation. Notes on Brazilian Mecoptera.

Penny, N. D., J. R. Arias, and H. O.-R. Schubart. 1978. Tendências populationais da Fauna de Coleópteros do solo sob floresta de terra firme na Amazônia. *Acta Amaz.* 8(2):259–266.

Pires, J. M., Th. Dobzhansky, and G. A. Black. 1953. An estimate of the number of species of trees in an Amazonian forest community. *Bot. Gaz.* 114:467–477.

Prance, G. T. 1973. Phytogeographic support for the theory of Pleistocene forest refuges in the Amazon Basin, based on evidence from distribution patterns in Caryocaraceae, Chrysobalanaceae, Dichapetalaceae and Lecythidaceae. *Acta Amaz.* 3:5–28.

Prance, G. T. 1977. The phytogeographical subdivisions of Amazonia and their influence on the selection of biological reserves. In G. T. Prance and T. S. Elias, *Extinction Is Forever*, pp. 195–213. New York: New York Botanical Garden.

Prance, G. T., W. A. Rodrigues, and M. F. da Silva. 1976. Inventário florestal de um hectare de mata de terra firme, km. 30 da Estrada Manaus-Itacoatiara. *Acta Amaz.* 6(1):9–35.

Procter, W. 1946. *Biological Survey of the Mt. Desert Region.* Part VIII. The Insect Fauna. Wistar Institute Press.

Ribeiro, M. de N. G. and Villa Nova, N. A. 1979. Estudos climatológicos da Reserva Florestal Ducke, Manaus, AM. III. Evapotranspiração. *Acta Amaz.* 9(2):305–309.

Richards, O. W. 1953. The classification of the Dryinidae (Hym.), with descriptions of new species. *Trans. R. ent. Soc. Lond.* 104(4):51–70.

Richards, O. W. 1978. *The Social Wasps of the Americas, excluding the Vespinae.* British Museum (Natural History).

Ross, E. S. 1970. Biosystematics of the Embioptera. *Ann. Rev. Ent.* 15:157–172.

Salmon, J. T. 1964. An index to the Collembola. *Bull. R. Soc. N.Z.*, no. 7.

Salt, G., F. S. J. Hollick, F. Raw, and M. V. Brian. 1948. The arthropod population of pasture soil. *J. Anim. Ecol.*, 17:139–150.

Saunders, P. T. and M. J. Bazin. 1975. *Nature, Lond.* 256:120–121.

Schade, F. H. 1973. The ecology and control of leaf-cutting ants of Paraguay. In J. R. Gorham, *Paraguay: Ecological Essays.* Miami, Fla.: Academy of the Arts and Sciences of the Americas.

Schubart, H. O.-R. and L. Beck. 1968. Zur Coleopterenfauna amazonischer Böden. *Amazoniana* (Kiel) 1(4):311–322.

Singer, R. and I. Araújo. 1979. Litter decomposition and Ectomy-corrhiza in Amazonian forests. I. A comparison of litter decom-position and ectomycorrhizal Basidiomycetes in latosol-terra-firme rain forest and white podzol campinarana. *Acta Amaz.* 9(1):25–41.

Stange, L. A. 1970. A generic revision and catalog of the Western Hemisphere Glenurini with the description of a new genus and species from Brazil (Neuroptera: Myrmeleontidae) *Contr. Sci.*, no. 186.

Stark, N. and Holley, C. 1975. Final report on studies of nutrient cycling on white and black water areas in Amazonia. *Acta Amaz.* 5:51–76.

Sterling, T. 1973. *The Amazon.* Amsterdam: Time-Life Books.

Steyskal, G. C. 1968a. 48. Family Micropezidae. In N. Papavero, *A Catalog of Diptera of the Americas South of the United States.* São Paulo: Universidade de São Paulo Press.

Steyskal, G. C. 1968b. 49. Family Neriidae. In N. Papavero, *A Catalog of the Diptera of the Americas south of the United States.* São Paulo: Universidade São Paulo Press.

Steyskal, G. C. 1968c. 54. Family Otitidae. In N. Papavero, *A Catalog of the Diptera of the Americas South of the United States.* São Paulo: Universidade de São Paulo Press.

Strickland, A. H. 1945. A survey of the arthropod soil and litter fauna of some forest reserves and cacao estates in Trinidad, British West Indies. *J. Anim. Ecol.* 14:1–11.

Takeuchi, M. 1961. The structure of the Amazonian vegetation. II. Tropical rain forest. *Jour. Fac. Sci. Tokyo Univ.*, III. 8(1):1–26.

Thiede, U. 1977. Untersuchungen über die Arthropodenfauna in Fichtenforsten (Populationsökologie, Energieumsatz). *Zool. Jb. Syst.* 104:137–202.

Val, F. C. 1976. Systematics and evolution of the Pantothalmidae (Diptera, Brachycera). *Archos Zool., Est. S Paulo* 27(2):51–164.

Vanzolini, P. E. 1973. Paleoclimates, relief, and species multiplication in equatorial forest. In B. J. Meggers, E. S. Ayensu, and W. D. Duckworth. *Tropical Forest Ecosystems in Africa and South America: A Comparative Review*, pp. 255–258. Washington, D.C.: Smith-sonian Institute Press.

Watson, J. A. L. 1970. Apterygota. In C.S.I.R.O. *The Insects of Australia*, pp. 217–223. Melbourne, Australia: Melbourne University Press.

Went, F. W. and N. Stark. 1968. Mycorrhiza. *Bioscience* 18(11):1035–1039.

Werner, F. 1962. Synopsis 189 (of address given at the Phoenix meetings of the Entomological Society of America). *Bull. ent. Soc. Am.* 8:161.

Wickler, W. 1968. *Mimicry in plants and animals.* London: Weidenfeld and Nicolson.

Williams, E. C., Jr. 1941. An ecological study of the floor fauna of the Panama rain forest. *Bull. Chicago Acad. Sci.,* 6(4):63–124.

Williams, W. A., R. S. Loomis, and P. de T. Alvim. 1972. Environments of evergreen rain forests on the lower Rio Negro, Brazil. *Tropical Ecol.* 13(1):65–78.

Willis, E. O.. 1976. Seasonal changes in the invertebrate litter fauna on Barro Colorado Island, Panama. *Revta bras. Biol.* 36(3):643–657.

Wolda, H. 1978a. Seasonal fluctuations in rainfall, food and abundance of tropical insects. *J. Anim. Ecol.* 47:369–381.

Wolda, H. 1978b. Fluctuations in abundance of tropical insects. *Am. Nat.* 112:1017–1045.

Wolda, H. 1980. Seasonality of tropical insects. I. Leafhoppers (Homoptera) in Las Cumbres, Panama. *J. Anim. Ecol.* 49:277–290.

Woodward, T. E., J. W. Evans, and V. F. Eastop. 1970. Hemiptera, *In* C.S.I.R.O. *The Insects of Australia,* pp. 387–457. Melbourne, Australia: Melbourne University Press.

Wray, D. L. 1967. *Insects of North Carolina,* third supplement. N. Carolina Dept. Agriculture, Division of Entomology.

Wygodzinsky, P. 1948. On two genera of "Schizopterinae" ("Cryptostemmatidae") from the Neotropical Region (Hemiptera). *Revta bras. Biol.* 8(1):143–155.

Wygodzinsky, P. 1966. A monograph of the Emesinae (Reduviidae, Hemiptera). *Bull. Am. Mus. nat. Hist.* 133:1–614.

Young, D. G. and G. B. Fairchild. 1974. Studies of Phlebotomine sand flies. Annual Report. U.S. Army Medical Research and Development Command, Washington, D.C.

Index

The italicized numbers indicate graphs or illustrations.